"The Yoga Service Best Practices Guide is the a
bringing yoga into school settings to promote
upon what we know about child development
practice, the book offers clear guidance on how
teens in school settings. I highly recommend this l

— PATRICIA JENNINGS, Professor at UVA Curry
School of Education, author of Mindfulness for Teachers

"This is a remarkable effort; a sage, inspiring, pragmatic and well presented manual of best practices for every one seeking to provide "safe, effective, inclusive, and sustainable" yoga classes in schools. The collective wisdom and experience is immediately apparent."

— JOHN KEPNER, Executive Director: International
Association of Yoga Therapists

"This is a thoughtful, well researched guide that should be an essential read for anyone wanting to bring yoga to schools. I'm so excited that the Yoga Service Council has been able to create a resource of this caliber using a collaborative model that leaves room for individual styles and philosophies. This is exactly what the field of yoga service needs- agreed upon best practices that unify all the great work already being done."

— HALA KHOURI, M.A. E-RYT, Co-founder Off the Mat,
Into the World, Somatic Counselor,
Yoga Teacher and Mother

"As a principal and superintendent I have implemented yoga programs in urban and suburban schools and have witnessed the success with students of all ages. Academics increase and off task behavior decreases with every yoga breath students take. *Best Practices for Yoga in Schools* is a great resource to start a yoga program in your school."

— CYNTHIA ZURCHIN, Superintendent of Schools, author
of The Whale Done School

"*Best Practices for Yoga in Schools* is a must have for anyone teaching or considering teaching yoga and mindfulness in a school setting. The book synthesizes an incredible body of knowledge and gives specific guidance in how to create effective programs that have lasting impact. I wish I had had this resource 20 years ago."

— MARIAM GATES, Director of Kid Power Yoga and author of
Good Night Yoga: A Pose by Pose Bedtime Story and Good Morning
Yoga: A Pose by Pose Wake Up Story

"A lot of very bright and experienced teachers, researchers, and clinicians gathered together and worked long and hard to create this well documented publication. For anyone who dreams to include the powerfully beneficial practices of yoga - such as movement, conscious breathing, and meditation, into any school curriculum, *Best Practices for Yoga in Schools* is an incomparable resource. To be effective and supported by the entire community, yoga must be introduced progressively and safely by well trained teachers. When offered in this manner yoga can be a powerful aid in helping students of all ages gain and maintain physical, psychological, and mental fitness, and manage stress. This book details how that can be accomplished."

— BERYL BENDER BIRCH, Co-Founder The Glve Back Yoga Foundation

YOGA SERVICE BEST PRACTICES GUIDE: VOL 1

BEST PRACTICES FOR YOGA IN SCHOOLS

Presented by the Yoga Service Council
and the Omega Institute

EDITORS

Traci Childress, MA and Jennifer Cohen Harper, MA

CONTRIBUTING EDITORS

Adi Flesher, M.Ed., Argos Gonzalez, M.Ed., Andrea Hyde, Ph.D., Wynne Kinder M.Ed.

CONTRIBUTORS

Candy Blaxter | Michelle Kelsey Mitchell
Bethany Butzer | Carol Kennedy
Lily Cavanagh | Sat Bir Singh Khalsa
Cheryl Crawford | Dee Marie
Anne Desmond | Allison Morgan
Lisa Flynn | Iona M. Smith
Lynea Gillen | Joanne Spence
Mayuri Gonzalez | Vanessa C.L. Weiner
Debby Kaminsky |

REVIEWERS

Carol Horton, PhD | Sat Bir Singh Khalsa, PhD
Patricia Jennings, PhD | Cynthia Zurchin, PhD

ISBN-10: 0692564713
ISBN-13: 978-0-692-56471-4

Suggested Citation: Childress, T., Cohen Harper, J. (Eds.). (2015). *Best Practices for Yoga In Schools*. Yoga Service Best Practices Guide Vol 1. Atlanta GA: YSC-Omega Publications.

Copy Editor: Jennifer Brown
Cover Illustrations: Karen Gilmour

CONTENTS

WELCOME TO THE FIRST YOGA SERVICE WHITE BOOK

The Yoga Service Council (YSC) and the Omega Institute for Holistic Studies are excited to introduce a series of white books that will establish best practices in the field of Yoga Service. This first White Book addresses yoga in schools. The second will address yoga for veterans.

The intention of each White Book is to be a resource for those who wish to share yoga practices in a way that is:

- safe, effective, and positioned in a broader social context;

- in touch with the relevant research; and

- respectful of the many intersecting realities found in any social setting, including the need for skillful relationship building within institutions.

We are tremendously excited for the opportunities that this series of White Books holds for making progress on our shared goal of helping to mainstream the practices of yoga and mindfulness in school systems, veterans' facilities, prisons, and other social institutions.

This particular White Book considers practices from several perspectives:

- individuals sharing yoga within their school;

- administrators of schools who are interested in incorporating yoga (or are being approached by those interested in doing so); and

- yoga teachers who teach (or want to teach) in schools.

This book is the work of 27 of the nation's leaders on yoga in schools—23 contributors and 4 reviewers. This group committed to an 18-month process of reviewing existing research and responding to surveys, which culminated in a working meeting at the Omega Institute in July 2014.

In addition to this group of experts, editors Traci Childress and Jennifer Cohen Harper drew inspiration from their many years of teaching children how to be healthy and well-balanced through yoga. They have put in countless volunteer hours to bring this research and practical advice to the public and to challenge a prevailing paradigm that is not always interested in or agreeable to introducing new experiences without hefty amounts of supportive evidence. If you want to give yoga a try in your school or if you already do, this White Book is for you.

We hope that this book serves you and your community well. If you would like to get to know us better, you can find us each May at Omega for our annual conference, or online at yogaservicecouncil.org

Yours in service,

Rob Schware
President, Yoga Service Council
Co-founder, Give Back Yoga Foundation

A MESSAGE FROM THE OMEGA INSTITUTE

Since our beginning, Omega's mission has been to awaken the best in the human spirit and to provide hope and healing for individuals and society. Yoga and service have always been core components of our offering and continue to serve as transformative tools toward our personal and collective growth and well-being.

Over the years, an ever-widening network of people and organizations that share our deep commitment to service have enriched our community. Through this experience we have learned that the power of working together is much stronger than walking the path alone. When we combine our energy and intentions, we extend our reach and have a greater positive impact in the world. That's why it's only natural the Yoga Service Council (YSC) and Omega have partnered together on a path to offer and support yoga service.

This partnership began in 2009, when Omega offered space for a group of yoga teachers to come together and talk about ways to support those who worked with vulnerable and underserved populations. The YSC emerged from this initial gathering and offered the first annual Yoga Service Conference at Omega in 2011.

During each Yoga Service Conference at Omega, we have discovered and rediscovered that the YSC board and the teachers who choose to be involved in this work are some of most compassionate people we have met. Yoga service truly is a practice of the heart—and it's a specific path of yoga that fully aligns with Omega's mission and ideals.

As a result of our shared commitment to yoga and service, the YSC and Omega decided to formally partner in 2014 to bring yoga into the lives of more individuals and communities who have limited access to these vital teachings. We are excited to announce this partnership and to continue working together with the YSC and all its member organizations.

One example of our partnership is the white book you are now reading, which is the first volume of in a series of white books on yoga service best practices. This project began in July 2014, when 23 leaders in the field of yoga in schools came together at Omega. We are thrilled to be able to support the work that is represented in *Best Practices for Yoga in Schools*.

We offer a special thanks to Rob Schware, Jennifer Cohen Harper, Traci Childress, and the entire YSC Board for their important work in the world. We're honored to be your partners on this journey.

With deep appreciation,

Robert "Skip" Backus
Chief Executive Officer

YOGA IN SCHOOLS: A SCIENTIFIC RATIONALE AND RESEARCH REVIEW

Dr. Sat Bir Khalsa

Children and adolescents in the U.S. face numerous life stressors in both family and school settings (1), which are known risk factors for mood and other psychological disorders (2). A recent U.S. survey suggests that the cumulative prevalence of psychiatric problems by age 21 exceeds 80% (3) with the majority of psychiatric conditions having child-adolescent onsets (4). There is a clear need for behavioral practices for improving social-emotional learning (SEL) and skills such as stress management and self-regulation in our children and adolescents. Despite historical calls for incorporating education of the whole child in our schools, including mental, emotional and physical health in addition to only academic skills (5), this has not been achieved, even though it is clear that academic and cognitive achievement is affected by, and dependent upon, student health (6). The modern education system is under pressure to focus on the academic performance of students, with few resources devoted to the health and wellbeing—physical, emotional and mental—of young people. Young adults complete their schooling with the training sufficient for obtaining employment, but often lack the skills crucial for maintenance of their mental health and well-being (7). Many educators, parents, and students argue for implementing instruction in such skills (7, 9, 12, 13).

Yoga is a multicomponent holistic system of practices that typically includes physical postures/exercises, breathing exercises, deep relaxation techniques, and meditation/mindfulness practices. Research on the potential benefits of yoga for adults and children has been growing in recent years (14), and research reviews suggest that yoga is efficacious for stress, mood and well-being (15-17). Yoga is also efficacious for children and adolescents yielding improvements in both physical and mental health (18-21). Yoga has psychological and physiological efficacy in enhancing three pivotal skills/attributes: mind-body awareness, self-regulation, and physical fitness, and these in turn can promote improvements in mental state, health, behavior and performance.

Increasing mind-body awareness leads to positive behaviors and outcomes as a result of an increased awareness of the rewarding feelings and positive experiences that occur with positive, healthful behaviors. Neurobiological evidence is now particularly strong for the role of yoga in improving stress management and self-regulation including emotion regulation (22). Finally, yoga enhances several aspects of physical fitness including neuromuscular coordination and strength, flexibility, balance and improved respiratory function. These three core skills (mind-body awareness, self-regulation, and physical fitness) with their ultimate positive outcomes on student behavior, mental state, health, and performance yield similar goals to those of school-based SEL programs, as defined by the Collaborative for Academic, Social and Emotional Learning (CASEL), whose goal is to address the underlying causes of students' problematic behavior while supporting academic achievement in K-12 school settings (8, 9), while they also add additional important life skills and competencies. Although mindfulness programs provide a key component of yoga, it can be argued that the additional physically based practices in yoga may actually serve to enhance and facilitate meditation/mindfulness while also adding improvements in psychophysiological functioning (23). The physical postures/exercises, breath regulation and relaxation techniques in yoga may be particularly relevant to facilitating contemplative practice in a young population that has high levels of psychophysiological energy and arousal and is not accustomed to sitting in stillness for extended periods of time. There is therefore a compelling rationale for the implementation of yoga in school settings (12, 24).

Accordingly, substantial interest is growing in the development and application of meditation/mindfulness- and yoga-based interventions in schools (12, 23, 25-27). Hyde (28) has noted recent government initiatives focused on educating the "whole child," and suggests that yoga in schools is an important component of this movement. There are a number of organizations that have come forward to support these initiatives, including the Garrison Institute, the Association for Mindfulness in Education, the International Association for School Yoga and Mindfulness and the Yoga Service Council. There has been substantial growth in meditation- and mindfulness-based interventions in schools (23). Yoga is being increasingly implemented in school settings (29). A recent survey of yoga programs in schools in the U.S. has revealed over 3 dozen formal yoga in school programs that are currently being implemented in over 900 schools across North America with over 5,400 instructors trained to offer yoga in educational settings (30). Despite variability in the detailed characteristics of implementation, training requirements, geographical regions served, and age ranges and schools, the majority of these programs share the implementation of the four basic elements of yoga (physical postures/exercises, breathing practices, relaxation techniques, and mindfulness/meditation) with a variety of additional educational, social-emotional, and didactic techniques to further enhance mental and physical health and behavior.

There is now a growing body of research on the efficacy of school-based contemplative practice programs (23). School-based mindfulness and meditation programs have been studied sufficiently to justify publication of a meta-analysis of 24 published studies, 19 of which were controlled trials, concluding that "mindfulness-based interventions in children and youths hold promise, particularly in relation to improving cognitive performance and resilience to stress" (31) in addition to a recent systematic analysis (32). Recently, Serwacki and Cook-Cottone conducted a systematic review of research studies of yoga in schools programs analyzing 12 published studies that assessed programs that were within the school curriculum, after school programs, and based at residential schools (33). Four of these studies were classified with special education populations, while the remainder included developing or at-risk youth. Most of the studies were in U.S. elementary schools, and were of low to moderate methodological quality. The authors concluded that the yoga programs yielded positive outcomes on factors such as emotional balance, attentional control, cognitive efficiency, anxiety, negative thought patterns, emotional and physical arousal, reactivity, and negative behavior.

More recent studies have described benefits of school-based yoga on psycho-social well-being factors on self-reported measures such as mood state (34), mood disturbance and negative affect (35), anger control (36), self-control (37, 38), aggression and social problems (38), fatigue (36), resilience (36, 37), self-regulation (39, 40), anxiety (35, 38, 41, 42), depression (42), problematic stress responses (43), self-awareness (37), self-esteem (44, 45), coping frequency (46), mental, social, and physical well-being (47), general distress, physical arousal, and hostility (42), and rumination, emotional arousal and intrusive thoughts (42, 48) and alcohol use (49). Beneficial effects have also been reported in teacher-rated factors including classroom behavior and social-emotional skills (50), concentration, mood, and ability to function under pressure (51), hyperactivity (52), student grades (53), attention, adaptive skills, behavioral symptoms, and internalizing symptoms (54) and social skills (49). Qualitative interview studies of yoga in schools instruction have indicated improvements in sense of calm, ability to focus, ability to control behavior under stress, and self-esteem (55), and greater kinesthetic awareness, stress reduction, mood management, and social cohesion (56). A few studies have examined physiological outcome measures, finding decreased cortisol concentrations (50), more stable breathing patterns (57), and improvements in heart rate variability (41) and stress reactivity as reflected in skin conductance responses (49).

Research on yoga in schools is a recent field that is still in its infancy, with currently fewer than about 50 published trials in peer-reviewed journals and with only 3 of these published before 2005. Not surprisingly, most existing studies are preliminary in nature and are of low to moderate methodological quality. The majority of existing studies have focused on elementary school students, many have small sample sizes, most have used self-reported subjective measures, most have not used comparison control groups, very few have used randomized controlled trial designs, almost none have evaluated optimal frequency and duration of instruction or long-term efficacy, and measurements of fidelity of implementation are generally lacking (58, 59). Furthermore, many of the positive results appear as trends rather than robust statistically significant changes and in many controlled studies only a few of the outcomes measured show positive changes (36, 45, 46) or no significant differences at all (60, 61), and two studies have found counterintuitive increases in negative mood state (60) and perceived stress (46). Finally, some studies that have examined both teacher- and student-rated outcomes have found significant effects for teacher, but not student, ratings (51, 54). Thus, the conclusions that can be drawn from these studies are tentative and should therefore be interpreted with caution.

Nevertheless, the evidence suggests that school-based yoga interventions show promise for enhancing positive behaviors, mental state, health, and performance. The high prevalence of psychological conditions in youth, coupled with the absence of rigorous and systemic whole child interventions, suggests that the implementation of yoga in schools would be of significant value. Schools are critical for the establishment of healthy lifestyle behaviors from an early age and implementing yoga in schools could have far-reaching implications not only for school health but also for society as a whole. Given that school education is legally mandated, yoga programs have the potential to provide a large-scale society-wide intervention that globally enhances physical, emotional and mental health, and contributes to positive student outcomes. It is likely, pending additional high quality research demonstrating the feasibility, efficacy, and cost-effectiveness of yoga in schools, that yoga will become a well-accepted and universal component of school curricula.

This white book publication is a significant step towards facilitating more formalized explorations around yoga in schools, and it is poised to support yoga practitioners and providers to engage in meaningful discussions with school teachers and administrators seeking to integrate yoga into educational environments.

Rationale and Research Review Citations

1. Ryan-Wenger NA, Sharrer VW, Campbell KK. Changes in children's stressors over the past 30 years. Pediatr Nurs. 2005;31(4):282-91.

2. Grant KE, McMahon SD, Dufy S, Taylor JJ, Compas BE, Piscitelli R. Stressors and mental health problems in childhood and adolescence. In: Contrada RJ, Baum A, editors. The handbook of stress science: Biology, psychology and health. New York: Springer; 2009. p. 359-72.

3. Copeland W, Shanahan L, Costello EJ, Angold A. Cumulative prevalence of psychiatric disorders by young adulthood: a prospective cohort analysis from the Great Smoky Mountains Study. J Am Acad Child Adolesc Psychiatry. 2011 Mar;50(3):252-61.

4. Kessler RC, Wang PS. The descriptive epidemiology of commonly occurring mental disorders in the United States. Annu Rev Public Health. 2008;29:115-29.

5. Terman LM. The hygiene of the school child. Boston: Houghton Mifflin Company; 1914.

6. Elias MJ. Schools as a source of stress to children: An analysis of causal and ameliorative influences. J School Psychol. 1990; 27(4):393-407.

7. Durlak JA, Weissberg RP, Dymnicki AB, Taylor RD, Schellinger KB. The impact of enhancing students' social and emotional learning: a meta-analysis of school-based universal interventions. Child Dev. 2011 Jan-Feb; 82(1): 405-32.

8. Kress JS, Elias MJ. School-based social and emotional learning programs: Navigating developmental crossroads. In: Sigel I, Renninger A, editors. Handbook of child psychology. rev. ed. New York: Wiley; 2006. p. 592-618.

9. Greenberg MT, Weissberg RP, O'Brien MU, Zins JE, Fredericks L, Resnik H, et al. Enhancing school-based prevention and youth development through coordinated social, emotional, and academic learning. Am Psychol. 2003 Jun-Jul; 58(6-7): 466-74.

10. CASEL. 2013 CASEL Guide: Effective Social and Emotional Learning Programs (Preschool and Elementary School Edition). Chicago IL: Author; 2012.

11. Social and Emotional Learning Core Competencies [Internet].; 2014 [cited 3/13/2014]. Available from: http://www.casel.org/social-and-emotional-learning/core-competencies/.

12. Davidson RJ, Dunne J, Eccles JS, Engle A, Greenberg M, Jennings,P., & Vago,D. Contemplative Practices and Mental Training: Prospects for American Education. Child Dev Perspect. 2012 Jun 1;6(2):146-53.

13. Diamond A. The evidence base for improving school outcomes by addressing the whole child and by addressing skills and attitudes, not just content. Early education and development. 2010; 21(5):780-93.

14. Jeter PE, Slutsky J, Singh N, Khalsa SBS. Yoga as a therapeutic intervention: A bibliometric analysis of published research studies from 1967-2013. J Altern Complement Med. 2015; (in press).

15. Sharma M. Yoga as an alternative and complementary approach for stress management: a systematic review. J Evid Based Complementary Altern Med. 2014 Jan;19 (1):59-67.

16. Pascoe MC, Bauer IE. A systematic review of randomised control trials on the effects of yoga on stress measures and mood. J Psychiatr Res. 2015 Sep; 68:270-82.

17. Li AW, Goldsmith CA. The effects of yoga on anxiety and stress. Altern Med Rev. 2012 Mar; 17(1):21-35.

18. Birdee GS, Yeh GY, Wayne PM, Phillips RS, Davis RB, Gardiner P. Clinical applications of yoga for the pediatric population: a systematic review. Acad Pediatr. 2009 Jul-Aug;9(4):212,220.e1-9.

19. Galantino ML, Galbavy R, Quinn L. Therapeutic effects of yoga for children: a systematic review of the literature. Pediatr Phys Ther. 2008 Spring;20(1):66-80.

20. Kaley-Isley LC, Peterson J, Fischer C, Peterson E. Yoga as a complementary therapy for children and adolescents: A guide for clinicians. Psychiatry (Edgmont). 2010;7(8):20.

21. Hagen I, Nayar US. Yoga for children and young people's mental health and well-being: research review and reflections on the mental health potentials of yoga. Front Psychiatry. 2014;5.

22. Gard T, Noggle JJ, Park CL, Vago DR, Wilson A. Potential self-regulatory mechanisms of yoga for psychological health. Front Hum Neurosci. 2014; 8.

23. Bostic JQ, Nevarez MD, Potter MP, Prince JB, Benningfield MM, Aguirre BA. Being present at school: implementing mindfulness in schools. Child Adolesc Psychiatr Clin N Am. 2015 Apr;24(2):245-59.

24. Butzer B, Bury D, Telles S, Khalsa SBS. Implementing yoga within the school curriculum: A scientific rationale for improving social-emotional learning and positive student outcomes. J Child Serv. 2015;In Press.

25. Jennings PA. Contemplative education and youth development. New Dir Youth Dev. 2008 Summer(118):101,5, 9.

26. Saltzman A, Goldin P. Mindfulness-based stress reduction for school-age children. In: Greco LA, Hayes SC, editors. Acceptance and mindfulness interventions for children adolescents and families. Oakland, CA US: New Harbinger Publications; 2008. p. 139-61.

27. Thompson M, Gauntlett-Gilbert J. Mindfulness with children and adolescents: effective clinical application. Clin Child Psychol Psychiatry. 2008 Jul;13(3):395-407.

28. Hyde AM. The Yoga in Schools Movement: Using Standards for Educating the Whole Child and Making Space for Teacher Self-Care. In: JA Gorlewski, B. Porfilio & DA Gorlewski, editor. *Using standards and high-stakes testing for students: Exploiting power with critical pedagogy*. New York: Peter Lang; 2012. p. 109-26.

29. White LS. Yoga for children. Pediatr Nurs. 2009;35(5):277-95.

30. Butzer B, Ebert M, Telles S, Khalsa SBS. School-based yoga programs in the United States: A survey. Adv Mind Body Med. 2015;In Press.

31. Zenner C, Herrnleben-Kurz S, Walach H. Mindfulness-based interventions in schools—a systematic review and meta-analysis. Front Psychol. 2014;5.

32. Felver JC, Celis-de Hoyos CE, Tezanos K, Singh NN. A systematic review of mindfulness-based interventions for youth in school settings. Mindfulness. 2015 02/12.

33. Serwacki ML, Cook-Cottone C. Yoga in the schools: a systematic review of the literature. Int J Yoga Therap. 2012;(22)(22):101-9.

34. Felver JC, Butzer B, Olson KJ, Smith IM, Khalsa SBS. Yoga in Public School Improves Adolescent Mood and Affect. Contemp Sch Psychol. 2014:1-9.

35. Noggle JJ, Steiner NJ, Minami T, Khalsa SB. Benefits of yoga for psychosocial well-being in a US high school curriculum: a preliminary randomized controlled trial. J Dev Behav Pediatr. 2012 Apr;33(3):193-201.

36. Khalsa SB, Hickey-Schultz L, Cohen D, Steiner N, Cope S. Evaluation of the mental health benefits of yoga in a secondary school: a preliminary randomized controlled trial. J Behav Health Serv Res. 2012 Jan;39(1):80-90.

37. Ramadoss R, Bose B. Transformative life skills: Pilot study of a yoga model for reduced stress and improving self-control in vulnerable youth. Int J Yoga Therap. 2010;1(1):73-8.

38. Parker AE, Kupersmidt JB, Mathis ET, Scull TM, Sims C. The impact of mindfulness education on elementary school students: Evaluation of the Master Mind program. Adv Sch Ment Health Promot. 2014 07;7(3):184-204.

39. Bergen-Cico D, Razza R, Timmins A. Fostering Self-Regulation Through Curriculum Infusion of Mindful Yoga: A Pilot Study of Efficacy and Feasibility. J Child Fam Stud. 2015:1-14.

40. Razza RA, Bergen-Cico D, Raymond K. Enhancing Preschoolers' Self-Regulation Via Mindful Yoga. J Child Fam Stud. 2013:1-14.

41. Bothe DA, Grignon JB, Olness KN. The effects of a stress management intervention in elementary school children. J Dev Behav Pediatr. 2014 Jan;35(1):62-7.

42. Frank JL, Bose B, Schrobenhauser-Clonan A. Effectiveness of a School-Based Yoga Program on Adolescent Mental Health, Stress Coping Strategies, and Attitudes Toward Violence: Findings From a High-Risk Sample. J Appl Sch Psychol. 2014;30(1):29-49.

43. Gould LF, Dariotis JK, Mendelson T, Greenberg M. A school-based mindfulness intervention for urban youth: Exploring moderators of intervention effects. J Community Psychol. 2012;40(8):968-82.

44. Sethi JK, Nagendra HR, Sham Ganpat T. Yoga improves attention and self-esteem in underprivileged girl student. J Educ Health Promot. 2013 Sep 30;2:55,9531.119043. eCollection 2013.

45. Telles S, Singh N, Bhardwaj AK, Kumar A, Balkrishna A. Effect of yoga or physical exercise on physical, cognitive and emotional measures in children: a randomized controlled trial. Child Adolesc Psychiatry Ment Health. 2013 Nov 7;7(1):37.

46. White LS. Reducing stress in school-age girls through mindful yoga. J Pediatr Health Care. 2012 Jan-Feb;26(1):45-56.

47. Chen DD, Pauwels L. Perceived Benefits of Incorporating Yoga into Classroom Teaching: Assessment of the Effects of "Yoga Tools for Teachers". Adv Phys Educ. 2014;4(03):138.

48. Mendelson T, Greenberg MT, Dariotis JK, Gould LF, Rhoades BL, Leaf PJ. Feasibility and preliminary outcomes of a school-based mindfulness intervention for urban youth. J Abnorm Child Psychol. 2010;38(7):985-94.

49. Fishbein D, Miller S, Herman-Stahl M, Williams J, Lavery B, Markovitz L, et al. Behavioral and psychophysiological effects of a yoga intervention on high-risk adolescents: A randomized control trial. J Child Fam Stud. 2015 06/12.

50. Butzer, B., Day, D., Potts, A., Ryan, C., Coulombe, S., Davies, B., Weidknecht, K., Ebert, M., Flynn, L., & Khalsa, S. B. S. Effects of a classroom-based yoga intervention on cortisol and behavior in second- and third-grade students: A pilot study. J Evid Based Complementary Altern Med. 2015;20(1):41-9.

51. Ehud M, An BD, Avshalom S. Here and now: Yoga in Israeli schools. Int J Yoga. 2010 Jul;3(2):42-7.

52. Klatt M, Harpster K, Browne E, White S, Case-Smith J. Feasibility and preliminary outcomes for Move-Into-Learning: An arts-based mindfulness classroom intervention. J Posit Psychol. 2013 05;8(3):233-41.

53. Butzer B, van Over M, Noggle Taylor JJ, Khalsa SBS. Yoga may mitigate decreases in high school grades. Evid Based Complement Alternat Med. 2015;ID 259814:1-8.

54. Steiner NJ, Sidhu TK, Pop PG, Frenette EC, Perrin EC. Yoga in an urban school for children with emotional and behavioral disorders: A feasibility study. J Child Fam Stud. 2013;22(6):815-26.

55. Case-Smith J, Shupe Sines J, Klatt M. Perceptions of children who participated in a school-based yoga program. J Occup Ther Sch Early Interv. 2010;3(3):226-38.

56. Conboy LA, Noggle JJ, Frey JL, Kudesia RS, Khalsa SBS. Qualitative Evaluation of a High School Yoga Program: Feasibility and Perceived Benefits. Explore. 2013;9(3):171-80.

57. Jensen PS, Stevens PJ, Kenny DT. Respiratory patterns in students enrolled in schools for disruptive behaviour before, during, and after Yoga Nidra relaxation. J Child Fam Stud. 2012 08;21(4):667-81.

58. Greenberg MT, Harris AR. Nurturing Mindfulness in Children and Youth: Current State of Research. Child Dev Perspect. 2012;6(2):161-6.

59. Feagans Gould L, Dariotis JK, Greenberg MT, Mendelson T. Assessing fidelity of implementation (FOI) for school-based mindfulness and yoga interventions: A systematic review. Mindfulness. 2015 04/12.

60. Haden SC, Daly L, Hagins M. A randomised controlled trial comparing the impact of yoga and physical education on the emotional and behavioural functioning of middle school children. Focus Altern Complement Ther. 2014;19(3):148-55.

61. Hagins M, Haden SC, Daly LA. A randomized controlled trial on the effects of yoga on stress reactivity in 6th grade students. Evid Based Complement Alternat Med. 2013;2013:607134.

AN INTRODUCTION FROM THE EDITORS

Traci Childress and Jennifer Cohen Harper

It has been an honor to work with so many dedicated people to bring this white book into being. From its inception, everyone involved came to the project with a deep commitment to the work of sharing yoga in schools. Creating this resource required us to explore ourselves, our work, our field, and many intersecting ideas and definitions. This challenged us, and we know this work will continue to challenge us as the field of yoga in schools evolves.

Yoga, as Sat Bir Khalsa points out in the forward article of this book, is a set of practices that support the development of self-awareness and self-regulation, along with improving physical and mental health outcomes for children. When taught in schools, high quality yoga programs have the potential to improve both student wellbeing and readiness to learn, as well as contribute to an improved school climate. Currently, we know of over 900 schools with official yoga programs. There are undoubtedly more, and many teachers and parent volunteers share yoga with children as well. These programs are growing steadily. With so many children experiencing yoga in school, it is critical that we work as a community to share information and build our capacity to offer programming that fully respects the needs of both students and schools.

The information offered in this white book is meant to support those who wish to share school-based yoga in ways that are safe, effective, inclusive, and sustainable. This includes yoga instructors and yoga service organizations, as well as school teachers and administrators, parents and the school community. Our hope is that this guidance, derived from the collective experience of the larger community, will benefit the children and be useful for those serving them.

The best practices outlined in this book are based on the knowledge of 23 contributors and their collective years of work in the field. You can find contributor biographies at the end of this book. As a new field, there is not yet extensive research to support every practice suggested here. However, we confidently offer these practices as a solid foundation from which the field of yoga in schools can grow. They are based on the collective wisdom and collaborative input of the paper's many contributors; preliminary research; the experiences of practitioners, teachers, and administrators; and research from related fields, including education, sociology, and child development. We hope this book fuels future research projects and helps articulate the nuanced questions that will stimulate scientific inquiry into school-based yoga.

In order to understand the context in which we put this book together, a brief overview of some core concepts and definitions follows, including how we define a "best practice," what we mean by yoga and yoga service, and how yoga in schools fits within those related frameworks.

The Relationship Between Yoga, Yoga Service, and Yoga in Schools

Sharing yoga in schools is a winding path that requires awareness and skill in many areas beyond the knowledge of how to teach yoga practices. To effectively and sustainably offer high-quality yoga programming in a school setting requires that we grapple with, and address head-on, the intersecting realities of the school environment.

To begin this conversation, we needed a clear definition of yoga. We chose to use a definition that reflects many yoga styles and that encompasses core practices that are often included in research on yoga's efficacy: yoga is a set of practices that includes postures or movement, breathwork, focused attention, and deep relaxation. We recognize that other aspects of yoga, including ethical, psychological, and philosophical study, may be an important component of some programs.

While this definition of yoga is helpful, we know that sharing yoga in schools involves more than just yoga. So, we chose to frame the discussion within the broader context of yoga service.

Yoga in Schools is Yoga Service

For this project, we used the working definition of yoga service first published by the *Huffington Post* in 2015 in an interview we (Traci Childress and Jennifer Cohen Harper) did with Rob Schware, Board President of the Yoga Service Council. It defines yoga service not by who is served, but rather by the manner in which the practices are offered:

Yoga service is the intentional sharing of yoga practices within a context of conscious relationship, supported by regular reflection and self-inquiry.

Teaching yoga in schools is first and foremost about teaching yoga to children and youth. Being in conscious relationship with students in this situation means being educated in youth development and able to adapt teaching techniques to the way children learn. All children do not experience and react to the world in the same way, and we must educate ourselves about the many things that can affect our students' experiences. We must be conscious of issues related to many factors, including culture, religion, race, socio-economic status, and language; have an understanding of specific needs and sensitivity to trauma history; be aware of how behavior management strategies affect students' sense of safety and self-confidence; understand how school culture and organizational mandates influence children; and more. Being in conscious relationship with students when teaching yoga in schools is much like being in conscious relationship with the entire world, as almost every facet of a society is reflected in its children. This is a complicated and challenging task, and undertaking it requires substantial reflection and self-inquiry.

When we step into a school, we step into a space that is shared by people with experiences and histories that may vary widely from our own. In order to be of true service, we must be willing to open our heart and mind to different perspectives and opinions, recognize our own assumptions and tendencies, seek out advisors and trusted colleagues who can help us hold ourselves accountable, and work to reduce barriers to meaningful relationships.

Combining knowledge of developmentally appropriate yoga practices, conscious relationship practices, and self-inquiry and reflection allows us to offer meaningful school-based yoga programs that have the potential to transform the educational environment, provide young people with tools to support their wellbeing, and help students thrive in a wide variety of situations.

What Are Best Practices? Why Are They Needed for School-Based Yoga?

The term "best practice" has been used to describe what works or is effective in a particular situation or environment.

A best practice is not:

- complicated,

- trying to prove a particular perspective or solve a research question,

- used to further one person's work or a particular program, or

- a marketed version of a practice.

Any school-based yoga program can, and should, have its own best practices. This book articulates more generalized practices that have application across programs and in a variety of contexts and can be utilized by anyone in the community. We also considered questions that might be relevant for the yoga in schools community or for future research, as we recognize that many questions remain unanswered in this work.

When we step into the school environment, we become responsible for other people's children. This responsibility demands that we connect to a body of work that is larger than our own. When we work as islands, we inevitably work with blind spots. One goal of collaboratively outlining these best practices is to empower us as we connect our work so that we can hold one another accountable for bringing yoga into schools with a shared level of understanding. In the end, the aim for the field must be bigger than the aim of our individual programs. Our goal must be to improve our understanding of how to share yoga with youth in schools in a safe, effective, and just way.

How This Book is Organized

This publication is a White Book, sometimes also referred to as a White Paper. A white book is a publication created by a group of experts in order to express an opinion, make a statement, or share knowledge. In this case, the experts come from the field of yoga and education. This publication lives in the context of research that supports its claims, but it most explicitly expresses the wisdom and knowledge that this particular group of contributors and editors were able to cull from their years of practice in the field. The intention of this publication is to be user friendly, concise, and when possible, to point readers to concrete references that relate, contextualize, and support the claims. It is also significant that this publication can work in reverse. By bringing experts together to articulate concise understandings they share about what works and what is important in the field, we are mapping out details of interest to the research world that can support the articulation of important research questions.

There were many contributors to this project. As editors, we (Traci Childress and Jennifer Cohen Harper) worked as both project developers and content editors: organizing the in-person gathering and related events, contributing and revising writing, collecting and synthesizing the input of other contributors, and organizing and editing the content. We worked with four outstanding contributing editors, whose roles were to review and revise content provided by contributors, as well as provide writing on relevant sections of the book according to their areas of expertise. Contributors attended the working meeting at the Omega Institute, helped to create content, and supported the editors throughout the revisions. The book was then evaluated by four reviewers who offered support and feedback before the final version you are holding was complete.

As we sought to integrate the ideas generated through our collaboration, the structure of this paper became clear. Prior to this introduction is an overview of the current research on yoga in schools, along with a scientific rational for offering school based yoga, written by Dr. Sat Bir Khalsa. Then the first four chapters examine overarching information relevant to all yoga service providers working in schools. In Chapter One, we discuss culture, communication, and getting programs set up in a way that maximizes sustainability. In Chapter Two, we explore the content of yoga in schools programs through some best practices relating to curriculum development. Chapter Three describes suggestions for staffing programs and training yoga teachers to work in school settings, and Chapter Four offers considerations for the legal requirements, safety concerns, and logistical matters that may arise.

In Chapter Five, we offer a deeper exploration of practices related to the cultivation of productive and mutually respectful relationships, both among adults and between instructors and students. This chapter examines more closely some of the ideas discussed in our description of conscious relationship, in recognition of the fact that it is our responsibility as a community to hold ourselves accountable and serve every child with clarity and compassion, regardless of their background or circumstance.

The final two chapters (Elementary Age and Early Childhood; Adolescence) examine working with students of specific ages and consider developmentally relevant information.

For clarity, throughout the book we refer to yoga teachers as *instructors*, and classroom teachers as *teachers*. When speaking about yoga based organizations, we refer to them as *providers*. In some contexts, the term provider is used to refer to yoga organizations and individual yoga instructors collectively.

At the end of each chapter, you will find that we have provided references, to highlight works that have inspired, supported or reported the work of the contributors.

The Promise of a Collaborative Approach

We are inspired by how this book's contributors came together, wrestled with hard questions, and identified some important issues for us to consider and evaluate as a community. We hope that we can commit as a field to delve into the questions, consider the discrepancies, look for synergies, and build relationships with research institutions, related fields, and one another.

We hope these suggestions serve you well. No teacher, program, or school can implement all of these best practices. Yet an awareness of the value of each one—and consideration of each best practice's significance to our individual work—will support us as we evolve. We invite you to join us in the process of reflecting on how our work relates to existing research and the larger community, and refining the questions we must ask of ourselves and each other in order to best serve our children.

CULTURE AND COMMUNICATION BEST PRACTICES

This section addresses ways to integrate yoga into a school community and create meaningful and effective systems of communication between organizations, individuals, students, and teachers. Because yoga may be unfamiliar to many individuals within a school community, clear communication is essential. Yoga providers need to be equally concerned with sharing accurate information and listening carefully to the concerns, questions, and needs of the community.

CULTURE AND COMMUNICATION 1:
COMMUNICATE WITH THE SCHOOL

Share information about the yoga program with the entire school community before and during the program.

The attitudes of the larger community (e.g. administrators, classroom teachers, aides, support staff, and parents) influence a program's efficacy and sustainability. Since the potential of yoga to support children may not be well understood, providers should be ready to explain what is being offered and provide an opportunity for community members to ask questions and become engaged in the program. Yoga providers should share information that makes all parties aware of the program's intentions, goals, and practical applications, as well as the specifics of what children will do during classes.

When sharing information with school staff, providers should establish expectations, clarify roles, and explore how school staff can support students' experience. This increases the capacity for school staff to support yoga instructors and vice versa, decreases misunderstandings and conflict in the classroom, and creates a more positive climate for students. A clear and mutually agreed upon strategy for frequent and consistent feedback between the outside provider and the classroom teacher will increase collaboration and communication for the duration of the program. Creating protocols for evaluating efficacy, making changes, and discussing issues will facilitate this process.

Community members should be provided with detailed text describing the yoga program, and, if possible, be included in a sample class. Providing information via multiple forums helps ensure that more people have access (e.g. electronically, as flyers, as printed letter for students to take home). Additionally providing sample classes at times when school employees and/or parents are more likely to attend will make them more accessible. When community members experience the practice themselves, they have an opportunity to gain insight about and understanding of the program or class, and to build relationships between the community and the yoga instructor.

Yoga has a rich, long history, and it may mean different things to different people. It is important for yoga programs to offer a clear definition of yoga in their materials, including the specific practices and techniques being used in their program. (See the introduction for the definition suggested by the editors). Instructors and providers should work to offer precise and conservative claims about what yoga can do/has done for schools, teachers, and students. Evidence for claims could come from program evaluations or assessments of learning, including participant feedback. But it is essential to make use of the growing scholarship on yoga programs, including the research cited in the introductory article of this white book.

A predetermined strategy for communication and collaboration between yoga providers and community members encourages:

- a culture of collaboration;

- mutual understanding of program and classroom needs;

- implementation of necessary changes;

- increased capacity to successfully navigate conflict, and

- successful and sustainable yoga programming in schools.

When sharing information with the school community, yoga providers should consider the following:

- Provide a definition of yoga and a general program description.

- Be prepared to answer questions about yoga and religion (See Curriculum 2).

- Concisely describe what will be done during the time that yoga teachers are on-site.

- List the potential benefits of the program and the evidence that supports these claims.

- Provide references for research that support the efficacy of school-based yoga programs.

Outline needs for the physical space (rooms, arrangements, equipment), and the scheduling and amount of time needed for each program component, including transition time and teacher preparation and/or breaks.

- Provide clear information about requirements and expectations, such as what students should or should not wear for yoga class.

- Provide contact information for questions and feedback.

CULTURE AND COMMUNICATION 2:
INTEGRATE YOGA INTO SCHOOL DAY

Integrate yoga into the school day and support participation by the entire school community.

In order to have the greatest impact and be of service to the most students, yoga programs should be integrated into the school day when possible, rather than exclusively taught as after-school programs.

Offering yoga during the school day, and integrating it into the school culture and curriculum, provides broader access to the experience, offers the potential to improve school and classroom climate, and extends the benefits of yoga to all students. If the goal is to create cultural change, it is useful to reach as many students as possible.

Incorporating yoga into the school day will reach the greatest number of students. Nonetheless, it is important to balance the desire to reach all students with the commitment to creating an invitational environment, where students do not feel pressured to participate in any activities that do not feel right to them (e.g. physical discomfort, emotional distress, lack of readiness, embarrassment), and that allows them to come to the practice in their own time. Even when individual students do not participate in all activities, they are becoming familiar with the concepts and gaining a greater understanding of what yoga is, and its benefit to them. Remembering that students can participate in different ways – e.g. through physical engagement, watching, thinking, or talking about an activity – can help teachers balance these best practices. Integrated programming also offers greater exposure to teachers and staff, and develops school staff's capacity to support practices even when the yoga instructor is not present.

Training teachers and school staff in yoga helps embed self-care and wellness in the culture of education, which supports both teachers and students. Yoga can be offered to school staff as a tool for self-care: a way to help manage the stress of the profession, reduce burnout, and maintain emotional balance in the classroom. Sharing yoga with school staff supports a broader cultural acceptance of the yoga program within the school and helps promote the recognition and reinforcement of the use of yoga-based tools by students throughout the day.

CULTURE AND COMMUNICATION 3:
ACCOUNT FOR THE SCHOOL'S NEEDS

Align program goals and success markers to the school's needs.

Different school communities have different missions, values, and needs. Different yoga providers and yoga programs are also designed to meet particular needs, and instructors have a wide variety of backgrounds, training, and experience. While there are many external influences that affect the efficacy of programming for a particular child, yoga programs will have a greater chance for success if programs are aligned with the stated goals and success markers of each unique school community.

Yoga providers should discuss with schools how program goals and outcomes may vary as a result of different implementation strategies. Soliciting information on the school's expectations for yoga programming, and what their goals for students might be, will allow yoga providers to better customize programming to meet the needs of the school. In some cases schools integrate yoga to meet measurable outcomes, in other times to meet a more general need, such as to fill an empty after-school programming slot, or to replace a PE class. Knowing the reasons that administrators or teachers hope to incorporate yoga will help providers to communicate about their on-going capacity to meet those needs.

Consider what the objectives of the yoga program are, and how both instructors and school administrators will determine whether or not those objectives are being met. As programs develop, requesting feedback from teachers and administrators is often the easiest and best way to get a quick and running check on how the program is going, how it is aligning to the school's needs, and if problems are developing.

References and Research Context

Chen, D. D., & Pauwels, L. (2014). Perceived Benefits of Incorporating Yoga into Classroom Teaching: Assessment of the Effects of "Yoga Tools for Teachers." *Advances in Physical Education*, 4, 138–148.

Davidson, R., Dunne, J., Eccles, J. S., Engle, A., Greenberg, M., Jennings, P., Jha, A., Jinpa, T., Lantieri, L., Meyer, D., Roeser, R., & Vago, D. (2012). Contemplative practices and mental training: Prospects for American education. *Child Development Perspectives*, 6(2), 146–153.

Henderson, A. (2001). Family-school-community partnerships 2.0: Collaborative strategies to advance student learning. Washington, D.C.: National Education Association. Retrieved from http://www.nea.org/assets/docs/Family-School-Community-Partnerships-2.0.pdf

Hyde, A. M. (2012). The Yoga in Schools Movement: Using Standards for Educating the Whole Child and Making Space for Teacher Self-Care. In J. A. Gorlewski, B. Porfilio & D. A. Gorlewski (Eds.), *Using standards and high-stakes testing for students: Exploiting power with critical pedagogy*. New York: Peter Lang Publishing, Inc. Retrieved from http://www.eric.ed.gov/ERICWebPortal/detail?accno=ED531347

Hyde, A., & Spence, J. (2013). Yoga in schools: Some guidelines for the delivery of district-wide yoga education. *Journal of Yoga Service*, 1(1): 53–59.

Institute for Educational Leadership. (2000). Strengthening partnerships: Community-school assessment checklist. Washington, D.C: Coalition for Community Schools and the Finance Project.

Jennings, P., Frank, J., Snowberg, K., Coccia, M., & Greenberg, M. (2013). Improving classroom learning environments by cultivating awareness and resilience in education (CARE): Results of a randomized controlled trial. *School Psychology Quarterly*, Sep 9 [Online First].

Khalsa, S. B. S., Hickey-Schultz, L., Cohen, D., Steiner, N., & Cope, S. (2012). Evaluation of the mental health benefits of yoga in a secondary school: A preliminary randomized controlled trial, *Journal of Behavioral Health Services & Research* (Vol. 38).

Marie, D., Wyshak, G., Wyshak G. H. (2006). Yoga Decreases Bullying in School. Retrieved from http://calmingkids.org/train-with-us/evidence-based-research-results

Marie, D., (2007). Yoga Increases Concentration in Elementary Age Students. Retrieved from http://calmingkids.org/train-with-us/evidence-based-research-results

Mendelson, T., Greenberg, M. T., Dariotis, J. K., Gould, L. F., Rhoades, B. L., & Leaf, P. J. (2010). Feasibility and preliminary outcomes of a school-based mindfulness intervention for urban youth. *Journal of Abnormal Child Psychology*, 38(7), 985–994.

Noggle J., Steiner N., Minami T., & Khalsa S. (2012). Benefits of yoga for psychosocial well-being in a US high school curriculum: a preliminary randomized controlled trial. *Journal of Developmental & Behavioral Pediatrics*, 3(3), 193–201.

Spence, J., & Hyde, A. M. (2012). Train-the-trainer: A white paper on the delivery of district-wide yoga education in Pittsburgh, PA. Pittsburgh, PA: Yoga in Schools. Retrieved from http://yogainschools.org/files/7714/2069/0586/YIS_White_Paper_Final_April_2012_1.pdf

Zurchin, C., Ballard, J., & Lacinak, T. (2012). *The Whale Done! School: Transforming a School's Culture Doing Things Right*. Bloomington, IN: Author House.

CURRICULUM BEST PRACTICES

Yoga programs vary in their specific content based on student needs, as well as the teacher's and organization's expertise. This chapter explores issues that have general significance to any yoga program in schools. No matter how well designed, no yoga program can reflect the needs of every individual child. As much as possible, however, providers must adapt sessions to meet the individual strengths, challenges, and circumstances of both individual students and the group as a whole.

See the chapters Adolescence and Elementary Age and Early Childhood for more information about programming and curriculum for specific age groups.

CURRICULUM 1:
CONSIDER EXISTING EDUCATION STANDARDS

Align a program's curriculum with existing national and state educational standards.

Yoga programs and schools should clearly define how the curriculum aligns with, complements, or supports national and state educational standards, as well as the goals of the individual school. Becoming aware of, and aligned with, education standards and goals supports program sustainability, creates a more collaborative climate, and improves the efficacy of yoga programming in schools. It is important to consider that different curricula may be needed for programs that address specific goals or students of different ages.

Administrators, teachers, and other key stakeholders are focused on ways to support their state, district, and school educational objectives, which are often tied to various forms of assessment and funding. Educators often feel that there are tremendous demands on their time, and may perceive a yoga program as competing with valuable instruction or preparation time. Integrating yoga thoughtfully into existing curricula encourages educators to view and use yoga as a support for achieving previously identified learning objectives.

Yoga programs are often used in schools to complement learning standards such as physical education, health and wellness, and social emotional standards. It can also be used to build skills—such as focused attention—that support learning in all subject areas. Providers should consider referencing research regarding both the relationship between contemplative practice and self-regulated learning, and between physical movement and learning.

CURRICULUM 2:
OFFER SECULAR PROGRAMS

Yoga programs should be secular in their approach and content.

Yoga service providers working in schools have an obligation to recognize and uphold the principles of secularism, and respect the diverse religious and nonreligious beliefs of the school community, both in principle and practice. Secularism maintains a separation between state and religious institutions, and recognizes religious equality before the law. Rather than promoting a position of non-belief, secularism invites the student to bring his or her own belief system to the educational experience.

A secular approach is maximally inclusive of all cultures and beliefs. It conforms to the legal requirements of the First Amendment, which maintains religious neutrality in public schools and their associated activities. Specifically, the Establishment Clause of the First Amendment prohibits public schools from advancing any particular religious belief over another, or over non-belief. The Free Exercise clause requires public schools accommodate the religious beliefs and practices of teachers and students where such practices do not interfere with the daily operation of the school. Because secularism maximizes inclusivity, this approach is recommended for private as well as public schools.

The question of how best to characterize the relationship between yoga as we know it in North America today and the historic yoga traditions of India has recently become more controversial. In 2010, the Washington, D.C.-based Hindu American Foundation (HAF) launched a well-publicized campaign to "Take Back Yoga" from what they saw as its excessive commercialism and cultural deracination. In 2013, a group of parents sued the public school system in Encinitas, California, because they believed that its district-wide yoga program was inherently religious, and therefore unconstitutional.

In 2015, the California Court of Appeals upheld the lower court's ruling that the Encinitas program was constitutional, stating that "while the practice of yoga may be religious in some contexts, the classes in question were "'devoid of any religious, mystical, or spiritual trappings." Notably, the HAF agrees that school-based yoga programs "should not . . . go beyond the instruction of asana and other physical components of yoga" to include religious practices or spiritual philosophies. Given that many training programs for adult yoga teachers today include loosely defined spiritual ideas and practices, it is critical to review both the design and implementation of school yoga programs to ensure they are consistently secular.

Yoga instructors should carefully consider how to introduce, plan, and deliver yoga programs in a public school environment. Specific ways to do this include:

- Be open and honest about the content.

- Seek to advance the interests of the community, including its most vulnerable members.

- Have an open conversation about religion rather than marginalizing any subgroup.

- Give parents and students the option to address concerns about the program; allow them to observe classes and ask questions.

- Avoid using practices that may cause confusion or misunderstanding, even if they are not explicitly religious (e.g. the use of Sanskrit, chanting, placing hands in prayer position).

- Allow students to opt out of any or all parts of the program. Have a planned opt-out process whereby students can be provided with an educational replacement if they are using the yoga program to meet a district or state requirement.

This area is particularly rich for continued research and conversation. Further discussion may include questions such as:

- What are the non-secular components, and potentially non-secular components of yoga?

- What are the components that may not have religious ties, but could be viewed as religious by particular communities?

- How do we learn how a community views yoga?

- How can we adapt program content and language to align with different cultures?

CURRICULUM 3:
USE A QUALITY CURRICULUM

Teach yoga classes from a high-quality and comprehensive curriculum.

Using a high-quality curriculum ensures clarity for yoga teachers and schools, and supports consistency for students. Quality curricula include comprehensive lessons that follow a predictable model and are connected to thematic units and the overall goals of the program.

High-quality curricula:

- clearly define goals and objectives;

- encompass all elements of yoga: movement, breathing, focused attention, and relaxation;

- scaffold lesson plans to build upon each other;

- integrate content that matches the age and needs of the specific audience, while allowing for variation based on student need and ability;

- offer parents and teachers resources for learning;

- consider practical time allotment for both the whole lesson and components of the lesson;

- include ways to asses students' understanding in the moment, which helps the instructor evaluate what students have internalized and make smart decisions about when and how to move forward in the curriculum (i.e. formative assessment);

- create ways for students to share feedback themselves (e.g. feedback box; reflection activities at the start or end of classes);

- offer adequate time for questions and requests for extra assistance;

- include closing and reflective activities and transitions between lessons, and

- have been developed and reviewed by experienced yoga teachers who are knowledgeable about child development and life in schools.

CURRICULUM 4:
SUPPORT POSITIVE
BODY IMAGE DEVELOPMENT

Support positive body image development in youth by including diverse ideas of health and beauty in school yoga programs.

Mainstream images of yoga have contributed to the cultural standard of what makes a body healthy and attractive. In the United States, this typically means slender (especially for women) and athletic (especially for men). Yoga programs in schools should intentionally work to remove language, images, and references that connect yoga to these limited ideas of health and beauty.

Yoga teachers can frame the practice in a broader context by emphasizing that yoga is not about outward body changes, while acknowledging that the physical body may change as a result of the practice. Though some people and programs include yoga as part of a weight-loss or healthy-weight maintenance program, it is generally more supportive to students to emphasize learning to listen to and recognize what the body needs.

Some guidelines to consider:

- When age-appropriate, consider having an explicit conversation about how yoga and yoga practitioners are viewed by society. With certain groups it may be possible to critically analyze and discuss images of yoga in the media.

- Emphasize how yoga offers a better understanding of, and relationship to, one's body, and to how one's capacity to notice what is happening in the body can increase through practice.

- Acknowledge that yoga can change the physical body, but that learning to listen to and recognize what the body needs is most important.

- Become familiar with the health and beauty norms held by school communities and individuals.

- Research the influence that specific yoga practices have on bodily states (e.g. the effect on heart rate, metabolism, stress, insomnia) in order to better communicate how yoga affects health and well-being.

CURRICULUM 5:
INTEGRATE PRACTICES TO DEVELOP SELF AWARENESS

Integrate practices to support self-awareness development into curriculum. Provide students with opportunities to check in with their own regulatory state before and during a yoga class.

Teachers should offer guided instruction for a brief check-in at the beginning of class (as well as throughout) to enhance students' experience and provide them with a life skill for outside the classroom.

Allowing students to take a few moments to notice their energy level, as well as their general physical and emotional state before starting a class supports them in developing self-awareness. When students increase their capacity to notice their heart rate, muscle tension, bodily sensations, breathing rhythm, balance, emotional state, and thought patterns, they can better perceive their own reactions to situations. Coupled with additional opportunities of noticing throughout a yoga class, students have the opportunity to observe the effects of yoga on their body and mind. Self-awareness is the first step toward self-regulation, and practices that support the development of self-awareness can help improve behavior in a way that is respectful, student-centered, and useful as a long-term life skill.

Self-awareness checklist:

- Physical check-in: Invite students to reflect on questions such as, "Are there aches, pains, discomfort, or sensations in your body? Are there areas of your body you are aware of? Is there tightness in any of your muscles?"

- Heart rate: Help students learn to notice the speed of their heart or their pulse.

- Breathing: Help students learn to notice the rhythm of their breath, and if they are breathing through their mouth or nose.

- Emotional state: Ask questions that help students notice how they are feeling.

- Thought patterns: Ask questions that help students notice their reactions or repetitive thoughts. Invite them to practice noticing and investigating, rather than judging their thoughts.

Recognize that increased self-awareness can at times lead to a recognition of intense emotion, including, negative, or even overwhelming, thoughts, feelings and sensations. As students build their capacity to tune in to their internal experience, consider how to respond to and manage the expression of feelings and emotions in a way that maximizes a sense of safety, is sensitive to potential previous trauma (see Relationship Building 6), and incorporates practices that support centering and grounding if needed.

CURRICULUM 6:
CONSIDER THE DEVELOPMENTAL APPROPRIATENESS OF PRACTICES

Teach practices that are safe for developing bodies.

When sharing yoga practices with children, instructors must take the developmental stage of students into consideration, including children's emotional, social, physical and physiological readiness for practices offered. Not all yoga poses or practices are safe for children. Generally practices that pose a threat to developing bodies should be avoided. Poses that require extensive strength or body awareness for safety should not be introduced to a general group unless those factors are well established; young bodies should be respected by providing poses that can develop balance and strength without risk of injury.

Headstand offers an example of a practice that should be avoided in school settings. Because the necks of children and adolescents are vulnerable, and because the practice of headstand requires the key physical strength of other muscles to insure a safe practice, avoiding it is the safe and recommended choice. When in doubt about the safety of a pose for a particular age group, do not teach it.

Similarly, some breathwork practices may not be safe for nervous systems in development and should be avoided. While slow, gentle breathwork is safe, there are many vigorous breathing practices that may not be appropriate for youth—particularly those that are forceful or require retaining (holding) the breath. Instructors should use simple, safe practices that do not demand extreme experiences, and encourage students to stop if they feel any discomfort, light-headedness, or difficulty breathing.

Yoga instructors should stay up to date on relevant research. As researchers further study the safety of particular practices, instructors can learn more about which specific yoga practices are effective for, or potentially harmful to, children at various stages of development. While this work is developing, instructors should teach only the practices that they are confident can be taught safely.

References and Research Context

Adams, M., Bell, L.A., & Griffin, P. (Ed.). (1997). *Teaching for diversity and social justice: A sourcebook*. New York & London: Routledge.

CAST. (2011). Universal Design for Learning Guidelines version 2.0. Wakefield, MA: Center for Universal Design for Learning. Retrieved from http://www.udlcenter.org/aboutudl/udlguidelines

Cohen Harper, J. (2013). *Little Flower Yoga For Children: A Yoga and Mindfulness Program to Help Your Child Improve Attention and Emotional Balance*. Oakland, CA: New Harbinger.

Cook-Cottone, C. P., Beck, M., & Kane, L. (2008). Manualized-group treatment of eating disorders: Attunement in mind, body, and relationship (AMBR). *The Journal for Specialists in Group Work*, 33, 61–83.

Flynn, L. (2013). *Yoga For Children: 200+ Yoga Poses, Breathing Exercises, and Meditations for Healthier, Happier, More Resilient Children*. Adams Media.

Flynn, L., & Ebert, M. (2013). Bringing yoga to the classroom: Tools for learning, skills for life. *Yoga Therapy Today*, Summer, 24–27.

Hyde, A. M. (2012). The yoga in schools movement: Using standards for educating the whole child and making space for teacher self-care. In J.A. Gorlewski, B. Porfilio & D.A. Gorlewski (Eds.), *Using standards and high-stakes testing for students: Exploiting power with critical pedagogy*. New York: Peter Lang Publishing, Inc.

Hyde, A., & Spence, J. (2013). Yoga in schools: Some guidelines for the delivery of district-wide yoga education. *Journal of Yoga Service*, 1(1): 53–59.

Klein, J., & Cook-Cottone, C. P. (2013). A systematic review of yoga for the treatment of eating disorders. *International Journal of Yoga Therapy*, 23, 41–50.

McTighe, J & Wiggins, G. (2005). *Understanding by Design*. Alexandria VA. Association for Supervision and Curriculum Development

Peck, D. (2014). Yes! Yoga for Encinitas students. [weblog] Retrieved from https://yogaencinitasstudents.files.wordpress.com/2014/09/yesyogarb.pdf

Roeser, R.W., & Peck, S. C. (2009). An education in awareness: Self, motivation, and self-regulated learning in contemplative perspective. *Educational Psychologist*, 44, 119–136.

Taylor, J. (2014). *The body image workbook for teens: Activities to help girls develop a healthy body image in an image-obsessed world*. Oakland, CA: New Harbinger Publications.

STAFFING AND TRAINING
BEST PRACTICES

Any education program is only as effective as its teachers. Therefore, the training and selection of yoga teachers will have a tremendous effect on the quality of any given program. Teaching yoga to children, and specifically teaching in the context of a school, is tremendously different from teaching yoga to adults. Both schools and yoga providers should carefully consider the training, experience, and expertise of instructors.

Teaching yoga in a school requires yoga expertise. It also requires knowledge of youth development and how to offer developmentally appropriate practices, the ability to engage a wide variety of students, an understanding of and capacity to manage challenging behaviors and group dynamics, and an ability to work collaboratively with classroom teachers and school staff.

STAFFING AND TRAINING 1:
HIRE QUALIFIED INSTRUCTORS

Schools and yoga providers should hire qualified instructors, specifically trained in children's yoga, to support the physical and emotional safety of students.

For the physical and emotional safety of students, instructors should always receive specific training in children's yoga. It is important that those working with children have training that includes youth development principles and behavior and classroom management. Yoga providers who train instructors should incorporate these aspects of the work into their programs.

One of the biggest influences on student learning is the quality of the instructor—their knowledge, experience, skill, and caring. Further training to meet the needs of the specific populations served in particular schools is recommended (e.g., trauma education, special education). Several sections of this white book provide specific recommendations for age groups (see Elementary Age and Early Childhood and Adolescence Chapters).

Sample checklist for assessing qualified instructors:

- Does the instructor have age-appropriate yoga training?

- Does the instructor have age- and issue-appropriate childhood development training?

- Does the instructor have first aid or CPR training?

- Does the instructor have behavior and classroom management training?

- Is the instructor aware of how to work with children with disabilities, trauma-related responses, and emotional and behavioral issues that may arise?

- Does the instructor have training in culturally responsive instruction?

STAFFING AND TRAINING 2:
STUDY CLASSROOM MANAGEMENT

Instructors should have training in classroom management strategies that are aligned with the goals of the yoga program.

It is the job of the instructor to establish trust and create and maintain a safe space to support learning, growth, and healthy emotional development for students. It is important for instructors to implement classroom management strategies that support this type of development. It is recommended that control-oriented or punitive methods be avoided as classroom management strategies, as these can shame or ostracize students. Classroom management practices should align with the larger goals of the yoga program, support mindful inquiry of students' experiences, encourage the development of internal discipline, and promote collaborative problem-solving and effective decision-making. Consider exploring the areas of social and emotional learning, restorative justice, mindful discipline, and positive discipline.

See more about behavior in Relationships Best Practice 1, and about the use of routines in Elementary Age and Early Childhood Best Practice 5.

Essential aspects of classroom management for a yoga teacher:

- Come to class ready to co-create agreements with students.

- Learn about what routines or rituals are already working for the school community.

- Clearly convey expectations to students.

- Ensure opportunities for questions and feedback.

- Maintain a connection to your own emotional experience when behavior challenges arise. Develop strategies to recognize emotions, calm them, and regain the capacity to act skillfully.

- Have a plan for how to help de-escalate conflict in the moment.

- Understand hot-button issues for each environment or community.

- Seek support and mentoring immediately when an event causes anger or fear, or when there is concern for the safety or well-being of a student or instructor.

STAFFING AND TRAINING 3:
TRAIN TO WORK WITH CHILDREN WITH DISABILITIES

Seek understanding regarding the experiences and specific needs of children with disabilities.

The Individuals with Disabilities Education Act (IDEA), passed in 1975, mandates the provision of a free and appropriate public school education for children and youth (ages 3–21) with a disability. Approximately 13% of children and youth receive special education services under IDEA. Over 50% of students who receive services were identified as having either a specific learning disability (i.e., a disorder in one or more of the basic psychological processes involved in understanding or using language, spoken or written, that may manifest itself in an imperfect ability to listen, think, speak, read, write, spell, or do mathematical calculations) or speech or language impairments. Smaller percentages of students received services for intellectual disability or developmental delay (13%), health impairments (12%), autism (7%), emotional disturbance (6%), and hearing impairment or blindness (2%).

During the 2011–2012 school year, about 95% of school age children served under IDEA were enrolled in regular schools, with the remaining 5% enrolled in special schools or programs. A growing number of students served under IDEA spend the majority of their day in inclusive classrooms.

As with all students, students with IDEA-identified disabilities are not a homogenous group. Seeking to understand these disabilities can support all educators.

The counselors, teachers, and/or mental health professionals who serve the school can be a good support as instructors look to differentiate instruction and curriculum to meet specific needs. Providers that offer children's yoga training should include information about working with students with diverse experiences and needs.

STAFFING AND TRAINING 4:
TRAIN INSTRUCTORS IN TRAUMA INFORMED PRACTICES

Yoga instructors need training in trauma informed practices, including a general understanding of the effects of trauma on children and adolescents.

Yoga instructors who work in schools should develop a basic understanding of the effects of trauma on children. (See related Best Practice Relationship Building 6). Training focused on understanding trauma and trauma sensitivity will better prepare instructors to respond to the needs and potential reactions of young people who have been exposed to trauma. Though it is not within the scope of a yoga provider in schools to treat children or to investigate specific situations, it is important to make teaching choices that assume some trauma is present.

Exposure to traumatic experiences in childhood—including non-direct experiences such as witnessing violent acts, and traumas related to neglect, abandonment or chronic stress—can substantially affect children's development. Instructors should have an understanding of, and sensitivity to, how trauma (the emotional response to experiencing a traumatic event) may manifest in their students' behavior and social interactions, and how it may influence experiences with activities offered in yoga classes.

Children who have experienced (or are currently experiencing) trauma, particularly in cases of abuse or neglect, are more likely to suffer from social, psychological, cognitive, and biological issues that make it difficult for them to regulate their emotions, pay attention, and form healthy relationships. They may exhibit a wide range of behavior, including, but not limited to, heightened vigilance, sensitivity to change in routine, increased impulsivity and reactivity, difficulty being still, withdrawal, or dissociation.

Instructors should take care to teach from a trauma-informed perspective. They should make every effort to avoid likely triggers (including touch), offer choices whenever possible, allow students to opt out of any practice, and respond with skill and compassion to behavioral challenges. Consistency and predictability are important parts of creating a sense of safety, and should be considered.

References and Research Context

Blaustein M, Kinniburgh K (2010) *Treating Traumatic Stress in Children and Adolescents: How to Foster Resilience through Attachment, Self-Regulation and Competency*. Guilford Press.

Cartledge, G., Gardener R, & Ford, D.J, (2009). *Diverse learners with exceptionalities: Culturally responsive teaching in the inclusive classroom*. In R. Gardner & D. Y. Ford (Eds.). Upper Saddle River, N.J.: Pearson.

Civic Enterprises, Bridgeland, J., Bruce, M., & Hariharan, (2013). *The missing piece: A national teacher survey on how social and emotional learning can empower children and transform schools. Collaborative for academic, social, and emotional learning*. Chicago: Author.

Goldberg, L. (2013). *Yoga therapy for children with autism and special needs*. New York, NY: W. W. Norton & Company Inc.

Harris, B. (2013). Building resiliency in students and teachers: Key ideas from research and practice. In A. Honigsdeld & A. Cohen (Eds.), *Breaking the mold of classroom management: What educators should know and do to enable student success*, Vol. 5. Lanham, MD: Rowman & Littlefield.

Jennings, P., & Greenberg, M. T. (2009). The prosocial classroom: teacher social and emotional competence in relation to student and classroom outcomes. *Review of Educational Research*, 79(1), 491–525.

Newcomer, L. (2009). Universal positive behavior supports for the classroom. OSEP Technical Assistance Center on Positive Behavior Interventions and Supports, 4(4), 1–16.

Meyer, L., & Chiang, R. (2012). Policies to promote safety and prevent violence. In National Association of State Boards of Education. Fit, healthy, and ready to learn: A school health policy guide. Retrieved from http://www.nasbe.org/project/obesity-prevention/fit-healthy-ready-to-learn-updated-release/

National Center for Education Statistics. Institute of Education Sciences. *Children and youth with disabilities*. Retrieved from http://nces.ed.gov/programs/coe/indicator_cgg.asp[AH1]

SAFETY, LEGAL, AND LOGISTICAL BEST PRACTICES

Understanding safety, legal, and logistical issues helps yoga providers craft protocols and practices to protect students' legal rights and safety. It also helps yoga providers understand how to meet the legal requirements of schools, and offers some awareness of how to address common logistical matters that affect a program's success.

For more practices that support the emotional, social, and physical safety of students, teachers and school staff, see the Relationship Building Chapter, as well as the Elementary Age and Early Childhood, and Adolescence Chapters.

SAFETY, LEGAL, AND LOGISTICAL 1:
KNOW SCHOOL POLICIES
AND PROCEDURES

Yoga providers should be familiar with school and classroom policies, procedures, and emergency protocols.

All schools and districts have specific safety policies and procedures that are important for yoga providers to understand and follow. Clear communication between school administration and providers is essential to promote the safety of people involved in programs, both in day-to-day activities and potential crisis situations.

Administrators should inform providers of all policies, procedures, and emergency protocols. Providers should seek out this information if it is not readily provided. This information should include procedures related to bathroom use, fire drills, lockdowns, medical emergencies, and weather events. Additionally, providers should be informed about policies and expectations for referrals for any mental health concerns and requirements for mandated reporting of child abuse. These plans should be communicated to both after school providers and providers working during the school day.

Yoga providers should ask for and receive information about:

- bathroom procedures,

- fire drills,

- lockdowns,

- medical emergencies,

- weather events,

- referral guidelines for mental health concerns or suspected abuse,

- a map of the building and a tour to identify exits and exit routes in case of evacuation

- policies and expectations related to liability and mandated reporting requirements in a school, and

- contact information for school staff, including who to contact in case of emergency.

SAFETY, LEGAL, AND LOGISTICAL 2: OBTAIN REQUIRED CERTIFICATES AND SCREENING

Yoga providers should have appropriate qualification, clearances, and insurance for working in schools.

Requirements for working in schools—including criminal background checks and adequate insurance coverage—should be discussed and agreed upon by the school and yoga provider. Districts vary in their requirements, but they must always follow federal and state mandates. Yoga service providers should be prepared to demonstrate the qualifications of their staff for working with students and teaching yoga to children. It may be desirable to have some previous experience working with the school's particular population (e.g., English language learners, students with disabilities, student athletes). Transparency regarding the screening process of yoga teachers increases confidence in the yoga program and promotes student safety.

All schools are liable for students in their care. Yoga providers working for schools as employees or contractors should ask schools about coverage for their staff while on-site, and what, if any, additional liability coverage is required or recommended. Instructors working as contractors for yoga providers should discuss this question with their organization. Though the school may have some liability in the event of an injury or incident during yoga class, providers should assume that they could be held liable for the negligence of their employees, contractors, and volunteers, and obtain appropriate liability insurance.

Consider requesting or providing the following:

- background check,

- FBI clearance,

- state criminal and/or child abuse check,

- drug screening,

- proof of liability insurance,

- instructor resume,

- certification of training,

- first aid/cpr certification,

- copy of driver's license, and

- references.

SAFETY LEGAL AND LOGISTICAL 3:
PREPARE FOR LOGISTICAL CHALLENGES

Yoga providers should identify and plan for potential logistical challenges caused by unexpected changes.

Logistical problems and other challenges are to be expected when working in a school environment. Schedule changes, weather closures, and absences are fairly common. School personnel are sometimes called away from planned activities to handle problems that arise in the moment. Students are sometimes pulled out of scheduled classes for individualized academic or social support, to prepare for sport or club activities or events, or for disciplinary measures.

These problems affect the duration and quality of time that yoga providers will be able to spend with students. Providers should check in with the school before and after each yoga session to see if there will be any changes in the schedule for that day or the day of the next session. Every school is different. Approach each school partnership as a unique relationship and discuss possible challenges with all stakeholders.

Always build some redundancy into communication structures and have a contingency plan for each part of a program or class. When potential problems are anticipated and discussed in advance, they can be more easily navigated. When a yoga provider is prepared for challenges, yoga programs will run more smoothly, and providers and administrators will have a more positive experience. Consequently, it's more likely that the program will continue.

Considerations:

- Who are the appropriate contacts within the school (e.g. for scheduling, health and safety issues, concerns about students)?

- Are there any issues that the school is dealing with that might strain or affect students' attendance? (e.g. a school play that many students are participating in; testing that demands extensive one-on-one meetings with specialists; an upcoming fire drill, standardized tests).

- What are notification policies if the school or instructor has to cancel a class? What is the policy for rescheduling?

- What is the payment policy in the event of a cancelled class?

- Who is authorized to remove a student from class, and under what circumstances?

SAFETY, LEGAL, AND LOGISTICAL 4: PLAN FOR PROGRAM SUSTAINABILITY

Consider factors that influence program sustainability when starting a yoga program.

The longer a school-based yoga program can be maintained, the better the chance that it will become a routine part of the school's schedule and students' lives. This makes sustainability a key goal for yoga programs.

In some cases, the most sustainable option for a school will be to have the school staff be trained to eventually take over the yoga programming. As responsible partners, yoga providers may remain consultants to school-based programs as long as they are needed. This model has the benefit of financial sustainability for the school and the possibility of yoga practices becoming integrated into the school more easily. However, this model does place additional demands on school staff, which may or may not be welcome, and may conflict with union regulations or job agreements.

In some cases, either due to lack of staff interest, capacity, or other barriers, the most sustainable option for yoga programming will be for a school to continue with an external provider while carefully and transparently planning for long-term funding needs. When mutually desired, administrators, service providers, and school board members can develop a concrete budget that supports long-term programming. Integrate planning for program sustainability into early conversations—don't wait until funding runs out.

Researchers are actively discussing the optimal frequency and duration (dosage) of yoga instruction and practice that maximize benefits. While this question is still being investigated, providers and schools can work together to observe student outcomes and make collaborative decisions about dosage. A prevalent suspicion is that frequency of practice is more important than the duration of each class. Just like any health, fitness, social-emotional learning, or anti-bullying program, it is likely that students and staff must continue practicing yoga—independently or as part of the school day—for ongoing benefit.

Conversations about funding sources might include these questions:

- How long is the school currently able to fund the program?

- What opportunities for future funding are available?

- How can the school and the yoga provider work together to ensure continued funding?

- What options are there for school staff to learn and teach yoga? Is there interest in this model?

Additional ways for yoga providers to support a sustainable yoga program:

- Provide perspective schools with a snapshot chart of pricing, class length, number of classes recommended, services offered, number of students reached, and cost per student.

- Create a protocol or written agreement for communicating and agreeing on clear expectations for a program with a given school. Be sure to have a system for revisiting and re-articulating the school's needs throughout the duration of the program.

- Be flexible; adjust program offerings based on need and budget concerns.

- Have a champion at the school, someone who can advocate for the program and influence others.

- Create a relationship with a funder, or draft a plan for financing the program over time.

- Identify clear strategies for increasing teacher and administrator buy-in.

References and Research Context

Coffey, J. H., & Horner, R. H. The sustainability of school-wide positive behavior interventions and supports. *Exceptional Children*, 78(4), 407–422.

Henderson, A. (2001). Family-school-community partnerships 2.0: Collaborative strategies to advance student learning. Washington, D.C.: National Education Association.

Hyde, A. & Spence, J. (2013). Yoga in schools: Some guidelines for the delivery of district-wide yoga education. *Journal of Yoga Service*, 1(1): 53–59. Available at http://yogaservicecouncil.org/wp-content/uploads/journal-of-yoga-service-spring-2013/

Institute for Educational Leadership. (2000). Strengthening partnerships: Community-school assessment checklist. Washington, D.C: Coalition for Community Schools and the Finance Project.

Oshinsky, J., & Dias, G. (2002). Liability of not-for-profit organizations and insurance coverage for related liability. The International Journal of Not-for-Profit Law, 4 (2–3). Retrieved from http://www.icnl.org/research/journal/vol4iss2_3/art_3.htm. 1

Schimmel, D., Stellman, L., & Fischer. L. (2011). *Teachers and the Law*. Boston: Pearson.

Shediac-Rizkallah, M. C., & Bone, L. R. (1998). Planning for the sustainability of community-based health programs: Conceptual frameworks and future directions for research, practice and policy. *Health Education Research*, 13(1), 87–108.

RELATIONSHIP BUILDING
BEST PRACTICES

This chapter describes best practices related to relationship building, both among the adults in a school community and between teachers and students. Relationships are one of the most significant factors in determining a program's success and must be considered carefully.

The following best practices draw from the framework of conscious relationship discussed in the Introduction. Being in conscious relationship involves acknowledging the many nuances of human experience. To exist in conscious relationship is to compassionately hold the truths about one another and the world in our interactions. It is an active attempt to see each person fully, honor each person's strengths, and acknowledge anything that is impeding the capacity to connect.

Educator Parker Palmer writes, "to teach is to create a space," and that when we teach, we always teach what we know. As teachers share yoga (or any other subject) with children, they create space for others to learn. They naturally offer the yoga practices and create their yoga programs through their own lens—from the perspective of their history, privilege, wounds, bias, assumptions, and wisdom. They offer yoga mixed with all the other things they know and have experienced in their lives.

Working with students in schools means that yoga instructors will invariably come into contact with children from a tremendously wide variety of circumstances. While no one person can be an expert regarding every possible situation, a baseline level of awareness, information, and sensitivity is necessary to protect students from misunderstanding on the part of the instructor, and even accidental harm that can stem from that misunderstanding. This chapter discusses how to become more sensitive to children by developing ways to become and remain connected to each child as an individual, in all circumstances, regardless of their behavior, label, or diagnosis. It also discusses ways to help create systems of accountability for yoga providers through a network of professionals and support people who can help to hold providers to a standard of higher excellence and help them see the full breadth of any situation.

A commitment to conscious relationship, supported by reflection and self-inquiry, allows yoga service providers to engage skillfully, honestly, and authentically with students and entire school communities, regardless of whether teachers and students come from similar life circumstances. It helps them look closely at what they know and don't know about themselves, those they serve and teach, and the communities they engage with. It trains them to better understand their own perspective and motivation, as well as those of their students, and to teach with the greatest clarity and efficacy possible.

RELATIONSHIP BUILDING 1: SEE ALL BEHAVIOR AS COMMUNICATION

Consider all behavior a form of communication. Understand that many things inform the way children experience and respond to an environment.

When children come to a learning experience, they seek a way to relate to it that feels safe. When their needs are not met, they seek ways to meet them. Children and youth of all ages are learning how best to relate to and learn in the world, and they may or may not have the tools they need to engage successfully in an environment or experience.

Sometimes, the attempt to find safety and comfort in a new environment or situation (and the people in it) can be perceived by adults as bad behavior or acting out, especially when an instructor does not have an extensive understanding of a child's background and/or needs. The most effective way to build a positive learning environment for all children is to assume that all behavior is an attempt to communicate an experience or need. The focus then can be on assessing what is being communicated and responding appropriately.

Children with learning or developmental disabilities, health problems, mental illness, or trauma may come to a learning environment with different needs—and different ways to communicate those needs—than their peers. In some cases, educators may be aware of the challenges a child is navigating; in other cases, children may have acknowledged or diagnosed disabilities (see Staffing and Training 3). Yoga instructors may be able to call on the expertise of school support staff or learn from research to craft the best learning environment for each child's needs. However, not all challenges are known or visible when working with youth. Therefore, providers need to seek ongoing education to support a broad understanding of students' experience, and how their teaching, actions, and presence may affect children's development and behavior.

Students who do not feel accepted or comfortable within the culture of a classroom for any reason may seek to avoid anxiety, discomfort, and fear through behaviors such as withdrawal or refusal to participate. In some instances, this might include particularly challenging behaviors, such as verbal or physical aggression toward peers or teachers. Instructors need to be prepared to respond appropriately to all behavior as a form of communication, rather than resistance or disrespect. Students are expressing an emotional experience or an unmet need. They are also trying to manage their internal environment with limited life experience, perspective and understanding, as well as limited capacity to regulate their emotions and reactions. Instructors can provide students with tools to meet those needs, and practices that support internal regulation of emotion and behavior.

When behavior is treated as communication:

- Children feel better understood and more supported.

- Instructors feel more confident and competent to address behavior.

- Classroom climate is more respectful, and teachers model care in relationship.

- Instructors respond with greater equanimity and flexibility to whatever arises in the class.

- Yoga and mindfulness tools can be taught and practiced in the situations in which they are most needed and useful—during difficult emotional experiences.

- The classroom is a safer space where students can learn and thrive.

RELATIONSHIP BUILDING 2:
COMMIT TO INCLUSIVITY

Commit to inclusivity and create space for differences (e.g., race, gender, language, religion, culture) to be discussed and honored in age-appropriate ways.

When working in the diverse context of public education, yoga providers and instructors must commit to inclusivity in programming and develop the capacity to offer classes that intentionally cultivate a safe environment for all students. Instructors should also be prepared to think critically about issues of difference and the associated issues of power and privilege, including identity privilege and group membership (e.g. religion, race, sex, gender, sexual orientation, wealth, ability, citizenship status, language, body size, or nationality.) Yoga providers will be more capable of offering inclusive programming if they are willing to examine how these issues influence their relationship with students, relationships among students, and their relationships with school communities, including parents and school staff.

Yoga in schools should be taught with awareness of creating a fully inclusive environment that is intentionally welcoming of all people. Below are some considerations, which may need to be adapted to suit each environment in which yoga is being taught.

- Be aware of religious, cultural, physical, and economic needs of students (and entire school communities), as well as their personal needs, sensitivities, and strengths.

- Look specifically at how "normal" is representative of the dominant culture and consider how this may be affecting your teaching and your students' experience.

- Understand that the social norms of any given community do not define the potential or personal individuality of a child. Get to know your students as individuals, as well as members of distinct social groups.

- Provide access to images of yoga being practiced by diverse populations (e.g. different ages, religions, abilities, genders, races, body types).

- Provide as many free options as possible for yoga practice, and work to ensure that buying special clothing and gear are not seen as essential to participation.

- Consider culturally responsive teaching strategies in your curriculum development and teacher preparation.

- Recognize when students from different backgrounds or with different abilities might experience specific postures or practices differently, and take that information into account when planning.

RELATIONSHIP BUILDING 3:
CREATE EQUITABLE RELATIONSHIPS

Create relationships that are fair, honest, and equitable, while maintaining appropriate boundaries.

Relationships are complex—at times yoga instructors may be perceived as playing a counseling role, while at other times, they may be seen as health care professionals and asked for medical advice. When students feel that their emotional experiences will be held without judgment, they may seek advice or support on a wide variety of topics outside the role and expertise of the instructor. Below are some considerations:

- Set and maintain professional boundaries while communicating care and compassion for student concerns.

- When in the role of yoga instructor, do not offer advice not related explicitly to the program being shared and its intended goals, even if you have additional knowledge or licensing.

- Recognize any desire to "save" students, and consider the problems that can arise from that framework of thinking.

- Don't make recommendations about health, family, or other concerns that fall outside of suggestions based on your area of expertise.

- Offer support, and when appropriate be an advocate and ally for your students instead of a fixer or saver.

- Know where to direct a student (e.g., school administrator or counselor) if he or she comes to you for physical or emotional support outside of the yoga instructor role.

Additionally, engaging in ongoing support from professionals in related fields, as well as from other yoga providers, will help instructors maintain clarity about appropriate boundaries and responses in their roles. It is essential to create and maintain relationships with, and learn from, allied professionals, particularly those already working in schools, such as school based social workers and counselors. Organizations that place yoga instructors in schools should consider what support instructors need in this area, and help them clarify boundaries when needed.

RELATIONSHIP BUILDING 4: PRACTICE SELF-REFLECTION

Yoga instructors should reflect on themselves, their teaching practice, experiences in the classroom, and relationships with students.

Yoga instructors' perceptions of themselves and their students are often incomplete or colored by their own emotional experience. Instructors should have a system in place to reflect on their own experiences, and assess successes and difficulties. This helps them see themselves and their students more clearly, and illuminates how to navigate challenges more skillfully.

It is critical for instructors to reflect on what happens in the classroom—including but not limited to challenging classroom moments—and ask what role their own perspective, biases, assumptions, and prior experiences might have played in the moment. A simple way to do this is for yoga instructors to set aside time after class to write down challenging moments or moments that did not go as planned, and actively ask themselves questions such as:

- What role did I play in this? What feelings was I experiencing in the moment?

- What role did the classroom environment play?

- What feelings might the child or children have been experiencing in the moment? Was I aware of those feelings at the time?

- What do I know about what was going on? What might I not know about the student or the situation that could inform my understanding?

- Was I feeling judgment of, or aversion to, the student in the moment?

- What can I change about my own response that might support a more respectful and effective resolution of a similar situation in the future?

Commit to maintaining a calm and equitable presence in the school environment. Reflecting on what is particularly upsetting, frustrating, or overwhelming helps teachers to develop self-care strategies, recognize when things are going awry, maintain a strong and grounded presence, and be consistent and skillful in responding to challenging behaviors. This self-awareness will help instructors manage strong emotions—in both students and in themselves—when they arise in class. Additionally, having a regular process for reflection will help instructors identify the role their own perspectives and experiences have on their perception of students' behaviors.

Moreover, instructors should understand their own history, particularly if they have a history of trauma, and recognize potential triggers that may arise in a classroom setting (e.g., certain types of behavior, language, sounds). Instructors should work to understand these reactions and minimize any effect they might have on students.

The art of following, supporting, and responding to students' needs is dependent on the emotional and energetic stability of the instructor. When students sense an instructor is calmly responding to their needs, they feel safer in the teaching relationship.

See Relationship Building 5 for suggestions about supportive peer groups and professional affiliations.

RELATIONSHIP BUILDING 5: DEVELOP RELATIONSHIPS WITH PEERS

Yoga providers should maintain relationships with peers, experts, and professionals in related fields.

Education is an interdisciplinary venture, especially within the context of K-12 schooling. Yoga providers should stay in touch with research and practice in other fields, such as, but not limited to, education, mindfulness, social and emotional learning, transformative education, and psychology and human development. Yoga instructors should connect with other professionals—counselors, social workers, occupational therapists and classroom teachers—for support, advice, and continued education.

Maintaining relationships across disciplines supports program efficacy and reflects a commitment to serving the whole child. Contact with allied professionals keeps yoga practitioners aware of practices that influence student experience, capacity to learn, and the culture of a learning environment. It also acknowledges the true complexity of teaching, and provides support to make teaching choices founded on accurate understanding of intersecting realities (e.g., social-emotional, cultural, physiological, developmental, psychological, situational).

Yoga providers should consider maintaining up-to-date lists of local professionals in allied fields who are willing to support the program and answer questions in their areas of expertise.

Schools would benefit from intentionally connecting yoga providers to school support staff such as school-based counselors, school-home liaisons and social workers, and occupational therapists.

Yoga instructors should also work with a local yoga-based organization that aligns with their values, and create relationships with similar national organizations. Peers and mentors are an important part of any profession, and can support the process of self-reflection discussed above. Organizational affiliation offers a form of accountability, in addition to resources for guidance and support.

RELATIONSHIP BUILDING 6: RECOGNIZE TRAUMA'S EFFECTS ON STUDENTS

Recognize that exposure to traumatic events often affects how children experience relationships, feel safe, and are able to integrate yoga practices.

Exposure to difficult or extreme circumstances that overwhelm a person's ability to cope (e.g. abuse, neglect, accidents, natural disaster) can result in an emotional response called trauma. Trauma can affect how children relate to others, what they perceive as a threat, and how their nervous system manages input from other people and the environment. Children who have experienced trauma at times may behave in ways that are challenging or confusing for other children and caregivers. Instructors need to be prepared to respond appropriately to these behaviors when working with children who have experienced traumatic events (keeping in mind that they may not have access to this information about a child's previous experiences, and that a large portion of the population has been exposed to traumatic events).

Below are some general suggestions for approaching work with children who have been exposed to trauma. Since much of the work on trauma-sensitive yoga has been limited to adult survivors (often of childhood trauma), yoga providers should think carefully and seek additional training about the differences in experience, adaptation, and behavior of children versus adults in this regard. This is particularly critical given that with children, the traumatic event is often ongoing, rather than in the past.

- Recognize that children who have been affected by complex trauma are often in a state of fight or flight that makes them more likely to perceive other people's behaviors as threats.

- Create predictable, calm environments and transitions. Since children affected by trauma are primed to see threat in their environment, they often experience novelty and transitions as particularly frightening and difficult.

- Avoid using touch for adjustments.

- Create, and pre-teach, a protocol for opting out of any part of the yoga instruction, such as closing the eyes or coming into specific postures. Make sure students are aware of their options, including opting out, and that they know where to go if they need to leave the room (and can do so safely).

- Avoid overpraising students who are always compliant, or who demonstrate what you consider to be good form. Always consider the message this sends to the group, as well as to the individual being praised.

- You cannot help anyone unless you are emotionally healthy yourself. Take care of your own needs, especially as they manifest in the classroom. Your ability to remain calm will have a tremendous effect on the students.

- Know your limits. Don't try to handle crises on your own. Always work closely with school social workers, counselors, or mental health professionals who know the individual child.

RELATIONSHIP BUILDING 7: COMMUNICATE WITH AND RESPECT SCHOOL STAFF

Understand and respect the role and responsibility of all school staff, including the classroom teacher, and communicate clearly when developing a program.

Teaching yoga in schools often involves complex relationships between the yoga provider and school staff, especially when classroom teachers are present for yoga practice. This relationship between yoga providers and classroom teachers is an important one, and can become challenging when there is misunderstanding or judgment. Yoga instructors who work in schools, whether as independent contractors or as part of an external organization, should work to understand and respect the responsibilities and needs of classroom teachers and other school staff. Ultimately, the permanent school staff—often the classroom teacher—is responsible for all of the instructional time, tasks, productivity, and evaluations of the students in her or his classroom, as well as their safety. In addition, classroom teachers care about their students and often feel protective of them, a feeling that may increase if what yoga instructors are offering is unfamiliar.

Yoga providers should seek to obtain as much general information about school and classroom culture and individual students' needs before programs start and prior to individual classes. While schools may not be able to disclose specific information about particular children, they may be able to make concrete and specific suggestions that will support a successful program.

Providers can ask questions such as:

- What do you need me to know about your class as a whole, and your students individually, before I offer my program? Are there any physical or behavioral concerns or contraindications? Do you have any concerns about the use of the classroom space?

- What do you need to know from me before I offer the program in your classroom?

- How does this offering affect your instructional time and required tasks? Are you interested in ways that yoga could help you in accomplishing those tasks?

- Did anything happen today that will potentially affect the children attending class?

- What are your hopes and concerns for your students? Could we think together about ways that the yoga program might support your objectives?

- Are you willing to participate on some level with the yoga education so that you can continue teaching yoga skills daily with your class? What would you need in order to feel comfortable practicing these skills with the students on your own?

In some cases, providers can get input from the families of children who will participate in a program by sending families a short introductory letter and information slip to fill out.

Some students may have specific plans (e.g., behavior plans and IEPs) and/or diagnoses that include protocols, accommodations, or contraindications for parts of the yoga practice. If students have support staff or aides, yoga teachers should understand that person's role when they are in the yoga class and establish realistic expectations based on that role. Support persons have concrete information about a particular student's needs. While they may not be able to disclose the reasons for their choices, it is best to defer to their input with children they work with directly. It is also appropriate to request a conversation with support persons to discuss the yoga instructor's goals, make recommendations aligned with her or his specific knowledge, and clarify what they can expect from the yoga practice. Have a point person at the school to support this relationship as needed.

When the yoga provider considers and seeks information about student needs, it:

- creates a safer environment for all of the children, classroom teachers, and yoga providers, minimizing potential misunderstandings and liability;

- supports respectful and compassionate classrooms;

- facilitates programs to run more smoothly; and

- allows programs to be more effective for those with specific needs.

RELATIONSHIP BUILDING 8:
BE AWARE OF THE CLASSROOM ENVIRONMENT

Be aware of the sensorial aspects of the space (e.g., lights, sounds, smells, textures, temperature) and their potential effect on students.

All children and the adults who work with them need a safe environment to facilitate learning. It is the yoga instructor and classroom teachers' roles to ensure that the unique needs of all of their students are met, including differently-abled and trauma-affected students. Some children are particularly affected by sensorial elements in the classroom and can have trouble focusing and/or communicating their needs as a result.

Being aware of lights, sounds, smells, textures, and temperature in the space makes it easier to address students' sensory needs. Being aware of a specific student's sensitivities and/or sensory processing challenges makes it easier to understand behaviors and responses that may seem inappropriate or confusing. Instructors cannot always control the environment and make it optimal for all students, so they do the best with what they have.

Simple changes that can help make a child who is struggling with sensory input more comfortable include:

- dimming or shutting off lights when possible (especially fluorescents);
- closing windows or shades;

- closing the door to the hallway, or using a white noise machine to muffle sounds; or

- moving desks and chairs out of the way so that students have as much personal space as possible.

A note of caution: what one student finds comforting another may find threatening. Seek the advice of the classroom teacher and support personnel who know the child best.

When providers understand students' sensory needs and do their best to address them:

- Children experience their needs as important and feel care and concern from the teacher.

- Nervous system reactivity decreases, and distraction is minimized.

- Some children have a greater capacity to participate in class.

- Students learn more about how their environment affects their emotions and energy.

- The yoga practice is more effective and enjoyable.

References and Research Context

Adams, M., Bell, L. A., & Griffin, P. (Ed.) (1997). *Teaching for diversity and social justice: A sourcebook*. New York & London: Routledge.

AFT (1999). The importance of staff 'buy-in' in the selection of proven programs. American Federation of Teachers. Washington, DC. Retrieved from http://rpdc.mst.edu/media/center/rpdc/documents/buy-in%20article.pdf

Binzen, M. (2010, April). Sensory integration and how yoga helps. [Web log]. Retrieved from http://www.yogachicago.com/mar10/mira.shtml

Childress, T. (2007). Power in Hatha Yoga communities and classes: Understanding exclusion and creating space for diverse cultures. *International Journal of Yoga Therapy, 17,* 51–56.

Childress, T (2007). Power in yoga professions: The implications of relationship and the necessity of accountability. *Yoga Therapy in Action,* 2007.

Cook, A., Spinazzola, J., Ford, J., Lanktree, C., Blaustein, M., Cloitre, M., et al. (2005). Complex trauma in children and adolescents. *Psychiatric Annals, 35*(5), 390–398.

Dorado, J., & Zakrzewski, V. (2013, October 23). How to help a traumatized child in the classroom. Retrieved February 2, 2015, from http://greatergood.berkeley.edu/article/item/the_silent_epidemic_in_our_classrooms

Dweck, Carol. (2007). The Perils and Promises of Praise. *Educational Leadership,* 65 (2) 34-39

Emerson, D., Sharma, R., Chaudhry, S. & Turner, J. (2009). Trauma-sensitive yoga: Principles, practice, and research. *International Journal of Yoga Therapy, 19,* 123-128.

Freire, P. (2006). *Teachers as cultural workers: Letters to those who dare teach.* (Expanded ed.). Boulder, CO: Westview Press.

Gay, G. (2000). *Culturally responsive teaching: Theory, research and practice.* New York: Teachers College Press.

Goldberg, L. (2004). Creative relaxation: A yoga based program for regular and exceptional student education. *International Association of Yoga Therapists, 14*(1), 68–78.

Goldberg, L. (2013). *Yoga therapy for children with autism and special needs.* New York, NY: W. W. Norton & Company Inc.

Garrison, J. (2010). Compassionate, spiritual, and creative listening in teaching and learning. *Teachers College Record, 112*(11), 2763–2776.

Guggenbuehl-Craig, A. (1971). *Power in the helping professions.* Dallas, Texas: Spring Publications.

Henderson, A. (2001). *Family-school-community partnerships 2.0: Collaborative strategies to advance student learning.* Washington, D.C.: National Education Association.

Howard, G. R. (1999). *We can't teach what we don't know: White teachers, multiracial schools.* Teachers College Press, New York.

Hyde, A. & Spence, J. (2013). Yoga in schools: Some guidelines for the delivery of district-wide yoga education. *Journal of Yoga Service, 1*(1): 53–59.

Jensen, P. S., & Kenny, D. T. (2004). The effects of yoga on the attention and behavioral of boys with Attention-Deficit/Hyperactivity Disorder (ADHD). *The Journal of Hyperactivity Disorders,7*(4), 205–215.

Jensen, E. (2008). A fresh look at brain-based education. *Phi Delta Kappan, 89*(6), 408-417.

Koenig, K. P., Buckley-Reen, A., & Garg, S. (2012). Efficacy of the Get Ready to Learn yoga program among children with autism spectrum disorders: A pretest-posttest control group design. *American Journal of Occupational Therapy, 66,* 538–546.

McIntosh, P. (2002). White privilege; Unpacking the invisible knapsack. In Rothenberg, P.S., *White privilege: Essential readings on the other side of racism.* (pp. 97–102). New York: Worth Publishers.

National Child Traumatic Stress Network, Secondary Traumatic Stress Committee. (2011). Secondary traumatic stress: A fact sheet for child-serving professionals. Los Angeles, CA, and Durham, NC: National Center for Child Traumatic Stress.

Nieto, S. (1999). *The light in their eyes: Creating multicultural learning communities.* Teachers College Press, New York.

O'Reilly, Mary Rose. (1998) *Radical presence: Teaching as contemplative practice.* Portsmouth NH: Boynton/Cook Publishers.

Palmer, P. J. (1998). *The courage to teach: Exploring the inner landscape of a teacher's life.* San Francisco, Calif.: Jossey-Bass.

Peck, H., Kehle, T., Bray, M., & Theodore, L. (2005). Yoga as intervention for children with attention problems. *School Psychology Review, 34*(3), 415–424.

Rogers, C. (2002). Defining reflection: Another look at John Dewey and reflective thinking. *Teachers College Record, 104*(4), 842–866.

Self-Reflection Questions for Teachers in Levin, B. (2001). *Energizing teacher education and professional development with problem-based learning.* Alexandria, VA: Association for Supervision and Curriculum Development.

Siegel, D. (2007). *The mindful brain: Reflection and attunement in the cultivation of well-being.* New York: W. W. Norton & Company.

Steps for mindful reflection and communication. In Dray, B. & Basler Wisneski, D. (2001). Mindful reflection as a process for developing culturally responsive practices. *Teaching Exceptional Children, 44*(1), 28–36.

Sumar, S. (1998). *Yoga for the special child.* Buckingham, VA: Special Yoga Publications.

Tyson, K. (2013, April 10). The importance of developing a common language. [Web log]. Retrieved on February 15, 2015, from http://www.learningunlimitedllc.com/2013/04/common-language/

Van der Kolk, B. (2014). *The body keeps the score: Brain, mind, and body in the healing of trauma*. New York: Viking Penguin.

Voss, A. (2014). *Sensory strategies for the classroom*. Retrieved from http://www.asensorylife.com/sensory-tools-and-strategies-for-the-classroom.html

ELEMENTARY AGE AND EARLY CHILDHOOD BEST PRACTICES

This chapter provides recommendations for working with early childhood and elementary age children. This includes children ages 2–10, generally described as preschool (ages 2–4) and elementary school (ages 5–10). This age range is a highly critical time and covers a broad spectrum of development: the brain, the body, fine and gross motor skills, social and emotional competencies that support children throughout their lives, and many foundational capacities.

Childhood is a time of exploration, experimentation, and curiosity. It is a natural period of learning, when children attempt to make meaning of their outer and inner worlds. During this time, students build a relationship with their body, thoughts, and feelings, and learn how to navigate the social world outside their home. Quality yoga programs for this age should seek to create an experience that is joyful and playful while being intentional about what to include and how to engage children in the educational process. The best yoga programs for young children harness the enthusiasm and natural curiosity of this time to maximize engagement and learning, and support children's growing capacity to self-regulate and manage their emotions.

Expectations of children's capacities vary widely, and educational settings, home, and societal perceptions of these capacities are not uniform. For example, some educational philosophies prioritize free play well into the elementary years, while others move into a more academic focus as early as kindergarten. These factors influence children and how they will respond to programs.

Yoga practice may give rise to a wide variety of experiences, sensations, thoughts, and feelings. Instructors can model—and children can practice—meeting these experiences with kindness, compassion, and curiosity. When yoga is taught in this spirit, it can help children befriend their body and mind and develop a sense of agency and competence independent of their peers or any standard measure.

Yoga providers working with children 10 and under must consider school and institutional expectations, and, to ensure success, be grounded in an understanding of the developmental considerations that influence children from the time they enter school (anywhere from ages 2–6) through the end of elementary school. Additionally, children enter educational institutions with varying degrees of school experience. A child may have his/her first school experience in kindergarten, first grade, or well before. Working with a group that is not homogenous in this sense can increase demands on educators and yoga providers, and require that they adjust expectations to accommodate students.

Children today often get the message that in order to do the right thing they need to conform to others' expectations (e.g., pass tests, follow rules, cooperate with the needs of a wide variety of adults). Yoga providers can and should provide a different experience in which children learn to value the internal messages from their bodies and minds.

Our culture prioritizes achievement and children often feel this pressure at a very young age. However, children learn best through activities that are aligned to their developmental capacities and inclinations. For young children this occurs through play or highly engaging experiences free of judgment or evaluation.

Early childhood yoga programs should consciously create an environment that:

- fosters a sense of inclusion, acceptance, and exploration;
- respects each individual student;

- allows life to move at the child's pace;

- encourages questions; and

- values self-discovery.

ELEMENTARY AGE AND EARLY CHILDHOOD 1: COLLABORATE WITH CLASSROOM TEACHERS

Develop relationships with classroom teachers. Encourage classroom teachers to participate in order to create a sense of safety for young children.

In order to create a sense of safety and clear expectations for students, adults in the classroom must have a positive, collaborative relationship and send consistent messages during class. Young children form attachment bonds with adults in their lives, and yoga instructors entering preschools and elementary schools will benefit from working with classroom teachers or school staff with whom children have likely already formed bonds.

Strong relationships between the adults in the room foster a sense of ease and safety during class, which allows students to feel comfortable enough to participate more fully. Prior to starting an early childhood or elementary school yoga program, consider an orientation meeting that includes the yoga instructor, classroom teacher, and any additional adults who will be present during class.

Topics to address include:

- expectation for participation;

- program goals;

- classroom management styles, goals, and expectations, including who will manage behavior challenges that arise during class;

- guidelines for how the adults in the room can engage in conversation or answer questions that come up during class; and

- ways adults can model safe modifications or make choices for themselves during practice if something isn't comfortable.

This initial meeting can also include sharing a simple introductory practice. It can also be helpful to set aside time for a mid-program assessment and check-in to develop a plan for the successful completion of the program.

Active participation by all the adults in the room (e.g., classroom teachers, aides, paraprofessionals) contributes to a supportive environment where everyone learns together. Lack of participation by the classroom teacher or other adults can limit students' engagement, which may make it harder for them to integrate the skills they're learning.

When teachers actively participate in yoga:

- students are encouraged to participate more fully and feel less like they are being watched or judged;

- students see a wider range of adults modeling ways to participate;

- students often feel safer;

- there is often stronger buy-in;

- teachers gain yoga experience and can reinforce the practice when yoga instructors are not present; and

- teachers can use practices for themselves.

Things to consider:

- It is important to offer modifications for adults with limitations and to discuss, in advance, how adults can model self-care by choosing to rest when a pose doesn't feel right.

- Clarity of expectations for participation is important for the instructor to establish with any other adults in the room. If the instructor has encouraged children to listen to their body and make good choices about their needs (e.g. resting in child's pose when tired, taking a break from a pose if it feels like too much, choosing not to do an activity that is uncomfortable) and the classroom teacher is attempting to help with classroom management by telling children who appear not to be fully participating to do the poses, the mixed message becomes very confusing for the students.

- Classroom teachers have very limited preparation time. Be clear on roles in the classroom—if yoga class has been included in prep-time, it may be unrealistic to ask teachers to participate. Building a respectful relationship is essential, and it may be helpful to communicate to students why their teacher cannot participate.

ELEMENTARY AGE AND EARLY CHILDHOOD 2: ENSURE PHYSICAL SAFETY

Align programs to realistic expectations based on children's developmental milestones in order to provide a physically safe experience.

The physical safety of students is essential and should be of primary concern for parents, schools, and yoga providers alike. Young children are developing fine and gross motor skills, coordination, and balance. Because most yoga programs entail physical activity, yoga educators in early childhood and elementary settings need to be aware of developmental milestones that determine the wide range of children's physical abilities at different ages. Utilizing child development resources that outline physical expectations according to age can be helpful when creating a yoga program.

In addition, maintaining a physically safe space requires yoga instructors to understand children's limited spatial awareness and the tendency for their movements to be big and enthusiastic. Placeholders such as yoga mats, tape on the floor, carpet squares, or other visual markers can help delineate space, giving everyone room to move freely without bumping into others.

Children may be prone to injury even when following the lead of an instructor. This is particularly true if their previous life experiences have encouraged them to keep their internal experience to themselves. Often children will follow an instructor's lead even if a particular pose is uncomfortable or painful. Yoga instructors should continuously offer a range of options and encourage students to back off from activities that do not feel right, rest when needed, and ask questions at any time.

ELEMENTARY AGE AND EARLY CHILDHOOD 3: CONSIDER SOCIAL AND EMOTIONAL NEEDS

Consider the social and emotional needs of the students in order to create a safe space for yoga and support healthy social and emotional development.

It is important to establish a safe learning environment, one that maximizes students' comfort and minimizes the social and emotional risks of making mistakes or stating unpopular opinions. This fosters a sense of community in which students feel valued and are willing to take academic, social and physical risks.

When students feel unsafe during yoga, they may be unable to participate fully in the class, absorb what is being taught, or remember the practices. Establishing clear procedures and boundaries while responding compassionately and skillfully to challenging situations creates a sense of safety in the classroom.

Ways to create a safe(r) space:

- Spend time on the first day establishing age-appropriate community agreements that students feel invested in. Consider exploring the question of what each member of the group needs in order to feel safe.

- If possible, choose a private practice space that reduces the ability of others to observe children during class to help reduce their self-consciousness and discomfort.

- Be consistent and predictable.

- Remember that all behavior is communicating a need. Choose behavior management approaches that demonstrate respect for students and consistently seek to recognize and meet their underlying needs.

- Support group safety through collaborative games and activities that are playful and light in tone.

- Avoid separating students from the group or removing them from the class unless all other options for intervention have been exhausted.

ELEMENTARY AGE AND EARLY CHILDHOOD 4: USE MUSIC INTENTIONALLY

Use music for specific purposes. Recognize when it may be a distraction.

Students in this age group often connect to learning through music. Music can help regulate the energy of a group. Singing together builds community and feelings of connection. Combining movement with music is fun and natural, and often helps students remember sequences of movement, which can make them more likely to practice with the group and on their own.

While there are many benefits to incorporating music into yoga classes, there are also times when music can become a distraction.

When incorporating music, consider the following:

- Use music for deliberate purposes.

- Provide time for quiet reflection and consideration.

- Recognize when children become distracted or overwhelmed by competing or intense stimuli.

- Be aware of the possible impact of music on your students' energy level.

- Note the direct and indirect messages and appropriateness of lyrics.

- Do not use music with Sanskrit words or references to Hindu deities, which are often found in music used during adult yoga classes.

- Watch for a break in the flow that may occur when the teacher manages the music.

ELEMENTARY AGE
AND EARLY CHILDHOOD 5:
BE CONSISTENT

Offer a consistent experience and use repetition intentionally.

Young children benefit from a consistent structure that allows for a degree of predictability and a clear understanding of procedures. Routines create a sense of safety to help children settle into learning.

Repetition makes lessons more effective for elementary age children. It helps them learn new skills and absorb and integrate information. Yoga practices are often new to students, and thoughtful repetition can help them become habits, making it easier to bring the practices into everyday life. Yoga teachers should provide students with the opportunity to explore different aspects of the same activity.

Additionally, when yoga programs are consistent and utilize repetition, classroom teachers and participating educators can better absorb what is being offered and build confidence in their ability to teach, share, and encourage yoga activities when a yoga teacher is not present.

While repetition is important, new activities should still be introduced through-out the school year or class series. In order to deepen understanding and support students to develop new habits, utilize repetition. Balance this with the integra-tion of new activities, which help to stimulate children's ideas and understanding of what is possible.

ELEMENTARY AGE AND EARLY CHILDHOOD 6:
USE CLEAR LANGUAGE

Use language that is clear, concise, and aligned with program intentions when teaching activities or addressing successes and challenges.

Young children respond best to clear instructions with as few words as possible. Use concise language with intentional pauses. Instructors should provide simple instructions rather than requests while making sure children know that if something doesn't feel right, they can and should stop. Likewise, they should avoid filler language, (e.g., tics like "um," "let's all," "why don't we"); complicated anatomical or alignment cues (e.g., "rotate your inner thighs, lift the arches of your feet"); or potentially confusing metaphors (e.g., "shine your heart forward").

The way instructions are delivered strongly influences cooperation and confidence. Too many instructions or requests may be confusing for young children. For children to integrate the information they receive, instructions need to be layered and appropriately spaced. This reduces confusion and allows the teacher to better gauge student understanding. It also creates space for students to listen for bodily sensations and cues.

Clear, thoughtful language is also important when providing commentary to celebrate successes in the class or address challenging moments. Instructors should use language that guides children but does not judge them, that offers information and provides clear feedback that describes what is working. A description such as "I see you are balancing on one foot," is more valuable than a more general phrase like "good job." Alternatively, when addressing a difficult situation or clarifying boundaries, choosing language that describes and teaches, rather than judges or shames, is more helpful. For example, instead of saying "Why are you walking on the yoga mat again with dirty shoes?" say "walking on the yoga mat makes it dirty."

ELEMENTARY AGE
AND EARLY CHILDHOOD 7:
MAKE TIME FOR RELAXATION

Ensure time for developmentally appropriate deep relaxation.

There is a tremendous need for down time in our overly stimulating world. Preserving space for relaxation during yoga sends a strong message that relaxation is as important as the other aspects of the practice. Many children struggle with sleep deficits and have a hard time both falling and staying asleep at night. According to the 2004 "Sleep in America" poll done by the National Sleep Foundation, sleep deprivation is a systemic problem: over 60% of children have sleep problems at least a few times in a week. Research on sleep loss in childhood demonstrates that it has a dramatic effect on learning and school success.

While many factors influence a child's ability to sleep well, teaching deep relaxation practices can help children get additional rest during the day and can be a valuable tool to help them fall asleep at night.

When offering relaxation practices, consider the following:

- Not all students will feel comfortable and safe closing their eyes—offer options to keep their eyes open (e.g. use a focus point, lower the gaze).

- Lying flat on the back can feel vulnerable. Not all students will be able to relax in this position—offer students a blanket or help them find a position that works for them.

- Offer guided relaxation practices like progressive muscle relaxation and creative visualizations in ways that leave students free to experience it for themselves. Avoid language that suggests an experience (e.g., instead of "notice how nice the cool air feels," instead say, "notice the feeling of the cool air on your skin" so students can decide for themselves how the air feels).

- Teach students to practice relaxation activities on their own so they can use them at home.

ELEMENTARY AGE AND EARLY CHILDHOOD 8:
USE PLAY

Use play to support learning, understanding, and development.

Play is the work of young children. It empowers them to learn and develop socially, emotional, and academically.

Providing ways for children to explore that are engaging and free of judgment or evaluation activates their curiosity and natural capacity to learn. A spirit of playfulness puts value on a child's experience and reinforces the importance of practice for its own sake. Opportunities for collaborative (non-competitive) play with others supports children as they develop their capacity to exist in a social environment and see themselves as a member of a community. Successful yoga programs for young children integrate play into the curriculum and encourage a spirit of playfulness in the teachers as well.

In early childhood settings, props can be used playfully to create meaningful and accessible classroom agreements and conflict management approaches. Props such as puppets, dolls, or stuffed animals can be an effective way to engage playfully with young children and examine broader ideas around conflict management. They can also be used to further develop ideas and concepts being explored in a yoga program (e.g., kindness, self-care).

Children of a young age will frequently seek to understand their world by acting out what they do not understand. Be aware that play such as superhero or weapon play has a developmental and social context. Adhere to school policies around what is and is not allowed, but avoid using language that might make children experience shame around their attempt to understand what they may be experiencing in their lives.

References and Research Context

Anderson-McNamee, J. K., & Bailey, S.J. (2010). *The importance of play in early childhood development.* Bozeman, MT: Montana State University.

Board of Trustees of the University of Illinois. (2009). The Importance of Fantasy, Fairness, and Friendship in Children's Play An Interview with Vivian Gussin Paley: *American Journal of Play,* 2(2), 121-138.

Bodrova, E., & Leong. D.J. (2001). Can instructional and emotional support in the first grade classroom make a difference for children at risk of school failure? *Child Development,* 76(5), 949–67.

Bransford, J., Brown, A.L., & Rodney, R. (Eds.). (2000). *How people learn: Brain, mind, experience, and school.* Washington, DC: National Academies Press.

Brown, B.B. (1990). Peer groups and peer cultures. In S.S. Feldman & G.R. Elliott (Eds.), *At the threshold: The developing adolescent* (pp. 171–96). Cambridge, MA: Harvard University Press.

Bruer, J. (1999). *The myth of the first three years: A new understanding of early brain development and lifelong learning.* New York, NY: Free Press.

Carlsson-Paige, N., & Levin, D. (1990). Who's calling the shots?: How to respond effectively to children's fascination with war play, war toys and violent tv. Gabriola Island, BC: New Society Publishers.

Chervin, R., & Mindell, J. (Eds.). (2015). ADHAD and Sleep retrieved from website of National Sleep Foundation, Retrieved February, 27, 2015 from http://sleepfoundation.org/sleep-disorders-problems/adhd-and-sleep

Cohen, J. (2010.) Teaching Yoga in Urban Elementary Schools. *International Journal of Yoga Therapy 20,*100-110.

Cohen Harper, J. (2013). *Little Flower Yoga For Children: A Yoga and Mindfulness Program to Help Your Child Improve Attention and Emotional Balance.* Oakland, CA: New Harbinger.

Darling, L. (2008). Songs, fingerplays, and movement activities for circle time. In L. Darling, Using the Mississippi Early Learning Guidelines: Complete curricula for three- and four-year-olds (Vol. 2). Mississippi State, MS: Mississippi State University Early Childhood Institute.

Dweck, Carol. (2007). The Perils and Promises of Praise. *Educational Leadership,* 65(2) 34-39.

Eccles, J.S. (1999). The Development of Children Ages 6 to 14. *The Future of Children,* 9(2), 30-44.

Faber, A., & Mazlish, E. (2012). *How to talk so kids will listen and listen so kids will talk.* New York, NY: Scribner.

Foundation for Child Development. (2006). *PK–3: What is it and how do we know it works?* New York, NY: Graves, B.

Foundation for Child Development (2006). *Core knowledge for PK–3 teaching: Ten components of effective instruction*. New York, NY: Sadowski, M.

Fromberg, D.P., & Bergen, D. (Eds.) (2006). *Play from birth to twelve: Contexts, perspectives, and meanings*. (2nd ed). New York, NY: Routledge.

Gordon, A.M., & Browne, K.W. (2013). *Beginnings & Beyond: Foundations in early childhood education*. Boston, MA: Cengage Advantage Books.

Hamre, B.K., & Pianta, R.C. (2005). Early teacher-child relationships and the trajectory of children's school outcomes through eighth grade. *Child Development, 72*(2), 625–38.

Hart, B. & Risley, T.R. (1995). *Meaningful differences in the everyday experience of young American children*. Baltimore, MD: Paul H. Brookes.

Heath, S.B. (1983). Racial and ethnic gaps in school readiness. In R.C. Pianta, M.J. Cox, & K.L. Snow (Eds.), *School readiness and the transition to kindergarten in the era of accountability*, (pp. 283–306). Baltimore, MD: Paul H. Brookes.

Heath, S. B. (1983). *Ways with words: Language, life, and work in communities and classrooms*. New York, NY: Cambridge University Press.

Kaiser, B. & Rasminsky, J.S. (2008). *Challenging behavior in elementary and middle school*. New York, NY: Pearson.

Isenberg, J.P., & N. Quisenberry. (2002). Play: Essential for all children. A position paper of the Association for Childhood Education International. *Childhood Education, 79*(1), 33–39.

Jones, G. (2003). *Killing Monsters: Why children need fantasy, super heroes, and make-believe violence*. New York, NY: Basic Books.

Kohn. A. (2011*). Feel Bad Education and other contrarian essays on children and schooling*. Boston, MA: Beacon Press.

Kohn, A. (1992). *No contest. The case against competition—Why we lose in our race to win*. Boston, MA: Houghton Mifflin.

Madsen, Jr., C.H., Becker, W.C., & Thomas, D.R. (1968). Rules, Praise, And Ignoring: Elements Of Elementary Classroom Control. *Journal of Applied Behavior Analysis, 1*(2), 139-150.

National Association for the Education of Young Children. (2009). Developmentally appropriate practice in early childhood programs serving children birth through age 8 (3rd ed.). Washington, DC: Carol Copple & Sue Bredekamp (Eds.).

National Association for the Education of Young Children. (2010). Cooperative games for preschoolers. Teaching Young Children, 4(2) 6-7.

National Center for Children in Poverty. (2007). Effective preschool curricula and teaching strategies. Pathways to Early School Success, Issue Brief No. 2. New York, NY: Brooks-Gunn, J., Rouse, C.E., & McLanahan, S.

Oghenetega, J. "What is a Safe and an Unsafe Space?" Academia.edu. Referenced from: http://www.academia.edu/7938423/WHAT_IS_A_SAFE_AND_AN_UNSAFE_SPACE. Retrieved on January 24, 2015, 8:35 A.M.

Paley, V.G. (2005). *A child's work: The importance of fantasy play.* Chicago, IL:University of Chicago Press.

Pica, R. (2011). Helping children cooperate. *Young Children,* 66(6) 60-61.

Sadeh, A., R. Gruber, and A. Raviv. 2003. Sleep, Neurobehavioral Functioning, and Behavior Problems in School Age Children. *Child Development* 73(2): 405– 417.

Saltzman, A. (2014). *A still quiet place: A mindfulness program for teaching children and adolescents to ease stress and difficult emotions.* Oakland, CA: New Harbinger.

Sameroff, A.J., & Haith, M.M. (Eds.). (1996). *The five to seven year shift: The age of reason and responsibility.* Chicago, IL: University of Chicago Press.

Selman, R.L. (1980). *The growth of interpersonal understanding.* New York, NY: Academic Press.

Smilansky, S., & Shefatya, L. (1990). *Facilitating play: A medium for promoting cognitive, socio-emotional, and academic development in young children.* Gaithersburg, MD: Psychosocial & Educational Publications.

Stevens, R. J., & Slavin, R. E. (1995). The cooperative elementary school: Effects on students' achievement, attitudes, and social relations. *American Educational Research Journal,* 32 (2) 321-351. http://aer.sagepub.com/content/32/2/321.abstract

Tate, A. (2003). Yoga and mental health: Children and adolescents make space in the system for deeper practices. *International Journal of Yoga Therapy,* 13, 83-87.

Wasserman, L. H., & Zambo, D. (Eds.). (2013). *Early Childhood and Neuroscience – Links to Development and Learning.* Dordrecht, Netherlands: Springer.

Zurchin, C., Ballard, J., & Lacinak, T. (2012). *The Whale Done! School: Transforming a School's Culture Doing Things Right.* Bloomington, IN: Author House.

ADOLESCENCE BEST PRACTICES

This chapter addresses teaching yoga to students in middle and high school who are approximately 11–18 years old. Adolescence is a time of tremendous change for students physically, and can be particularly intense emotionally. Providing effective and engaging yoga programming for youth at this age requires that yoga providers recognize both the unique strengths and potential challenges of adolescence, including adolescents' need to develop greater independence from parents, teachers, and other adults.

Adolescence is a time when children are deeply engaged in self-discovery and exploring the inner workings and capacities of their identity. This natural inclination provides an opportunity for yoga teachers to make the experience of learning and practicing yoga more meaningful. This is also a sensitive time for young people—choices often have more significant consequences than they previously did, and the natural drive towards greater autonomy can at times compromise their relationships with adults in their life.

Yoga can be a healthy vehicle for the self-exploration that is central to adolescence. It is important that yoga programs working with adolescents offer students time to ask questions and talk about their experiences, both with the instructor and with each other. Effective yoga programs offer a tool-based approach that explicitly addresses how to use the practices in daily life. These practices have the ability to support adolescents in making healthy and productive choices during a period of life in which both risk-taking and vulnerability are high.

ADOLESCENCE 1: UNDERSTAND THE ADOLESCENT MIND

Develop an understanding of the developmental reality of adolescents and recognize potential challenges that may arise as a result.

As yoga providers seek to engage adolescents in yoga practice, they will benefit from keeping in mind what Dr. Daniel Siegel describes, in his 2014 book, *Brainstorm*, as the qualities of the adolescent mind: novelty seeking, social engagement, increased emotional intensity, and creative exploration. Often these qualities are assigned negative implications by adults, e.g. novelty seeking means risk-taking, social engagement equals rejection of adults, emotional intensity means impulsive overreaction, creative exploration implies rebelliousness. However, instructors must embrace their upsides (as described below based on Siegel's work) in order to maintain a positive attitude toward, and relationship with, adolescent students.

Along with an increase in risk-taking, novelty seeking leads to a desire to explore life and try new things. Social engagement might have downsides in the way of peer pressure and a changed relationship with parents. However, the drive for connection can also lead to strong community building and collaboration. Increased emotional intensity can lead to increased sensitivity and empathy, as well as a greater enjoyment of life. While creative exploration may lead to a rejection of the status quo, it also makes possible new ways of seeing the world, and can foster openness to possibility. This is a vibrant time of life, and the big energy of adolescence must be embraced.

Remember that questioning and pushing away from adults is important at this time, and not a sign that something is wrong with an adolescent or that they are disrespectful. Peer relationships take on more significance, and need to be respected and honored. Considering what is being asked of students in relationship to their peer networks is essential. Instructors can engage students most effectively by providing choices and building relationships. By honing their own capacity to connect with young people as individuals, instructors can assess what aspects of the practices will be most relevant to them.

Working with adolescents can be challenging. Instructors have to navigate not only the challenges they face, but their own relationship with their younger years. In working with adolescents, instructors must remember that while they may look grown, and are navigating increasing expectations, they are not adults. Youth need the security of clear minded, competent instructors who are firmly on their side, setting boundaries and creating safe spaces for exploration.

ADOLESCENCE 2:
SUPPORT HEALTHY
IDENTITY FORMATION

Reinforce healthy identity formation by creating a space that is inclusive, safe, and welcoming.

Adolescents are actively forming their identity and working to develop a clear sense of self by exploring their values, ethics, racial and ethnic identity, sexual orientation, sexuality, and gender identity. As such, this is a time of self-consciousness, and self-centeredness. While they are learning what makes them unique, they also have an increased need to "fit in." This leaves them vulnerable to peer pressure. Peer pressure—a part of life for everyone—can be an especially strong influence during the teen years, when peer relationships are so important to one's identity. Instructors must be sensitive to peer pressures and their potential negative impact on identity formation. Instructors should aim to create a positive space where students feel safe and welcome.

Peer pressure is not always bad. Good friends can encourage teens to do well in school, express themselves fully, get involved in positive activities, volunteer, eat healthy foods, and avoid drugs, alcohol, and other risky activities. Friends also help teens learn good social skills and better ways to communicate and work out problems. Negative peer pressure is when teens feel pressured to do something that doesn't support their own well-being, or when they feel judgment or bias for being their authentic self. Teens may be tempted to give in to negative peer pressure when they want to be liked or fit in, are afraid of being made fun of, or want to try something other teens are doing.

Peer pressure will remain part of a teen's life into adulthood. Therefore, the more that a yoga class can offer experiences that assist students in getting better at communicating their needs and boundaries, and supporting their peers, the better. Specific techniques to do this include:

- Encourage respectful language and behavior in the classroom.

- Tell students early and often that if something hurts, feels uncomfortable, or just doesn't feel right, they can stop. It's always appropriate in yoga to take a rest, slow down, or decide to do something different. Support these choices. Encourage students to share how they feel. Let them know it's OK to ask for assistance if needed.

- Offer instruction and modeling for ways to communicate and support healthy boundaries in poses that are done with partners so students engage with each other in a mutually supportive and respectful manner.

- Consider offering alternative activities for youth who aren't comfortable engaging in partner-based activities (See Adolescence 6).

- Use gender-neutral language in your teaching. Avoid gendered language and stereotypes; don't assume that your students identify as either female or male. Avoid using gendered language in classes, e.g., "this is a good pose for women," or "men may find this pose easier because…" Avoid statements or jokes that imply gender bias.

ADOLESCENCE 3:
CREATE A SAFE SPACE

Create a safe space by being aware of factors that encourage adolescents' mental health.

Yoga providers should work to support a positive and nonjudgmental environment that considers the changes taking place in the adolescent brain and encourages connection and well-being for youth. This is particularly critical given that mental health in adolescence can have effects that extend well into adulthood.

The National Association of School Psychologists offers a list of ways to encourage mental well-being for adolescents, including:

- Create a sense of belonging.

- Promote resilience.

- Ensure a positive and safe environment.

- Teach and reinforce positive behaviors and decision-making.

- Encourage youth to make a difference through helping others.

- Support physical health.

- Educate all involved about symptoms of mental health concerns.

Providers should consider factors that play a large role in the life of adolescents, including but not limited to:

- social pressures,

- sexual development,

- identity development,

- academic challenges, and

- family dynamics.

Because of the many explorations and changes in the life of an adolescent, safety is essential. In order for adolescents to feel safe, providers must have clear intentions and offer space for questioning. Working with this age group can be a balancing act—structure and clarity provides a sense of safety, but the natural inclination for exploration makes flexibility essential as well. For example, when choosing to teach challenging poses to youth, an instructor is providing a chance for adolescents to engage in risk, which is appropriate. However, at the same time, the provider must take care to have first established a learning space that is physically and emotionally safe for this exploration. There is a fine line between what is challenging and what is threatening, and it may not be possible to know each student's personal limits. Any work with this age group must hold these paradoxical realities at the forefront of the endeavor at all times.

Safe spaces are developed over time as students and teachers learn to trust one another and accept efforts and expressions (words and actions) in a nonjudgmental way. Mistakes and failures are an acceptable part of the process of learning, and need to be explicitly discussed when working with adolescents.

ADOLESCENCE 4:
ADDRESS STUDENTS' NEEDS

Be aware of, and responsive to, the emotional and physical needs of students in the present moment.

When creating curricula and lesson plans for adolescents, it is important to remember that students will engage most fully with practices that seem relevant to them in the moment. It is also critical for them to develop trust that instructors are attuned to them and respectful of their circumstances. Instructors must be able to adapt to the situation at hand and modify plans to reflect the present-moment needs of students.

By shifting the activities to fit the needs presented or observed, yoga instructors model how these practices can be used for self-care. By encouraging students to reflect on how they are feeling, and helping them learn what practices might support them, instructors are building students' capacity to respond to their own needs. For example, if students come into class exhausted, the teacher can explore a practice to raise energy or one that creates space for rest and recuperation. If students arrive with chaotic or scattered energy, it offers an opportunity to explore whether grounding work would be supportive, or if high-energy movement would be more helpful. Students will learn how to choose yoga tools for themselves by witnessing an instructors' willingness to explore options. By honoring their needs, adults can teach adolescents that their needs have value and relevance.

Adolescents are often receptive to learning more about what is happening in their brains and bodies from a scientific as well as experiential perspective.

As research is published that outlines the physiological effects of yoga poses, breathing practices, and relaxation techniques, yoga instructors should consider sharing this information with their adolescent students. When choosing to integrate information of this kind, it is essential to also acknowledge that individual students may not have a particular experience in a pose, just because research has shown that it is a standard response. Instructors must remember that people do not all experience practices in the same way. For example, what feels calming for one student might be agitating to another. Two-way communication and clarity of intention is important, as are discussions about contraindications, including the tendency to over-do and over-reach, even when it's not in our best interest.

ADOLESCENCE 5: ENCOURAGE SELF-DIRECTED PRACTICE

Offer instruction to help students create an independent practice by including practices to help them navigate challenges in daily life.

Adolescents, through school-based yoga programs, can learn to use yoga techniques as viable strategies to employ when they experience challenges, frustration, and stress. Yoga practice is particularly useful for adolescents because it doesn't need a large amount of time or space to be effective.

Instruction geared toward self-directed, independent practice can help adolescents see yoga as a life skill, rather than an extracurricular activity. For greatest benefit, yoga practices can be extended beyond the in-school yoga sessions in the following ways:

- Encourage student-centered conversations about how the practices can be used in everyday life (e.g., falling asleep at night, taking a test, calming down when upset).

- Suggest at-home practice logs (targeted to short, simple, sustained practices).

- Host parent/guardian-student educational events where parents or guardians and their children can practice yoga together. Include educational materials on ways to practice at home.

- Suggest or provide educational materials in a variety of media to support everyday practice (e.g., newsletters, apps, mp3s, videos).

ADOLESCENCE 6:
BE DISCERNING WHEN TEACHING PARTNER WORK

Be deliberate and cautious when offering partner poses or other activities that involve physical contact between students.

Some of the benefits of teaching partner poses (practices in which two students work together to support each other in a yoga postures) to teens include developing listening skills, building relational trust, and creating ally identities, all of which support social and emotional learning. However, partner poses should be offered with discernment, and not offered until relationships have been built and trust established.

Teachers may or may not have information that would be essential to creating safety around partner work, such as a student's history. For this reason, if offered, partner poses should be optional and opportunities for peer pressure related to participation in such activities should be minimized. Offer complementary activities that students can practice independently if they choose to forgo partner work, and create space for students to discuss their feelings and questions about partner poses. Consider showing videos or photos of teens doing partner poses, and let students hear or read what other teens have to say about partner poses—when such resources are available—so students have a clear understanding of what is being offered as they decide how to participate.

Allow adolescents to choose their own partner rather than assigning partners. Understand that instructors do not always know gender and sexual identities of students. Safety cannot be guaranteed—and may in fact be hindered—if the instructor attempts to partner students based on gender.

Consider what consent means in the context of partner poses, and actively work with students to create guidelines for asking permission to touch, and for accepting or rejecting touch. Partner work offers an opportunity to practice building skills around consent and can reinforce the idea that just because touch is meant to be supportive or helpful doesn't mean it's welcome, and that the person receiving the touch is always in charge, regardless of the intent of the giver. All students should communicate with each other during partner poses, and should clearly understand that they can ask for or reject physical contact during any part of the experience.

ADOLESCENCE 7:
AVOID PHYSICAL TOUCH

Carefully consider the use of touch, its implications, and issues of consent in yoga practice. Avoid touching students.

Physical touching with student consent is an accepted vehicle in many adult yoga classes for adjusting or enhancing yoga poses. Touching an adolescent student, even with their consent, is not recommended in a school environment.

Yoga postures should be taught in a way that increases the students' awareness of their own body and its needs, and helps them recognize their capacity to manage and use their body. When an instructor adjusts poses, students may receive a message that they are not doing the poses correctly, are not good at the practice, or need an external source to adequately control their body. Better choices than physically adjusting an adolescent include:

- verbally cuing adjustments to poses in cases where there is a safety concern;

- coming out of the pose, and re-entering it with more specific instructions;

- offering an opportunity to explore another aspect of a pose.

Touch that supports relaxation (such as hand or foot massages) is also an unnecessary risk, and not recommended. Consider that consent to be touched can be difficult to confirm when working with adolescents. Students at this age are vulnerable. As they develop awareness around their sexuality and consent issues, they may struggle to articulate what they are comfortable with. There may be social pressures to either be touched—or not be touched—that influence their decisions in a yoga space (e.g., if they feel that the instructor will be offended or hurt, or that their participation in class will be questioned by their decision not to be touched).

Often in a yoga studio environment, students are given the chance to opt out of being adjusted or physically assisted in poses. This opt out is not a strong enough stance when working in schools. Instructors should consider that students might not hear the invitation to opt out: they might be self-conscious making a decision that is different from the group, or assume that physically being adjusted is the default and opting out means doing something less than the full practice. Consciously or unconsciously, they may feel that they don't have the right to make decisions about their own body.

To prevent harm to students, misconceptions around sexual harassment, or other misunderstandings, touch is not recommended. When teaching in a school environment, it is better to minimize anything that could potentially exclude or harm a student. Choosing to avoid physical touch is always a safe and appropriate decision.

References and Research Context

AAP. (2014, August 25). Let them sleep: AAP recommends delaying start times of middle and high schools to combat teen sleep deprivation. Retrieved 3/5/2015, 5:19 pm from https://www.aap.org/en-us/about-the-aap/aap-press-room/Pages/Let-Them-Sleep-AAP-Recommends-Delaying-Start-Times-of-Middle-and-High-Schools-to-Combat-Teen-Sleep-Deprivation.aspx

APA. (2014, February 11). American Psychological Association survey shows teen stress rivals that of adults. Washington, DC: American Psychological Association. Retrieved from http://www.apa.org/news/press/releases/2014/02/teen-stress.aspx

Arch, J. J., & M. G. Craske. 2006. Mechanisms of mindfulness: Emotions regulation following a focused breathing induction. *Behavior Research and Therapy* 44, 1849–1858.

Benson, H., Wilcher, M., Greenberg, B., Huggins, E., Ennis, M., Zuttermeister, Myers, P., & Friedman R. Academic performance among middle school students after exposure to a relaxation response curriculum. *Journal of Research and Development in Education,* 33(3), 156–165.

Brown, R. P. MD, & Gerbarg, P. L. MD. (2012). *The healing power of the breath.* Shambala Publications.

Cacioppo, J. T. (1994, March). Social Neuroscience: Autonomic neuroendocrine, and immune responses to stress. *Psychophysiology,* 31(2), 113–28.

Childress, T. (2007). Power in Hatha Yoga communities and classes: Understanding exclusion and creating space for diverse cultures. *International Journal of Yoga Therapy, 17,* 51–56.

Childress, T (2007). Power in yoga professions: The implications of relationship and the necessity of accountability. *Yoga Therapy in Action,* 2007.

Cook-Cottone, C. (2013). Dosage as a critical variable in yoga therapy research. *International Journal of Yoga Therapy,* 23, 11–2.

Duncan-Ricks, E. N., C.S.W. (1992, August). Adolescent sexuality and peer pressure. *Child and Adolescent Social Work Journal,* 9(4), 319–327.

Emerson, D., & Hopper, E. (2011). *Overcoming trauma through yoga: Reclaiming your body.* Berkeley, CA: North Atlantic Books.

Feinstein, S. (2009). *Secrets of the teenage brain: Research-based strategies for reaching and teaching today's adolescents* (2nd ed.). Thousand Oaks, CA: Corwin.

Frank, J. L., Bose, B., & Schrobenhauser-Clonan, A. (2014). Effectiveness of a school-based yoga program on adolescent mental health, stress coping strategies, and attitudes toward violence: Findings from a high-risk sample. *Journal of Applied School Psychology,* 30(1), 29.

Gruber, E., & Grube, J. W. (2000). Adolescent sexuality and the media: A review of current knowledge and implications. *Western Journal of Medicine,* 172, 210-214.

Hyde, A., & Spence, J. (2013). Yoga in schools: Some guidelines for the delivery of district-wide yoga education. *Journal of Yoga Service*, 1(1): 53–59.

Illinois Enhance Physical Education Task Force. (2013). Illinois Enhance Physical Education Task Force: Recommendations and report – Executive summary. Springfield, IL: Illinois State Board of Education. Retrieved from http://www.isbe.net/EPE/html/EPETF.htm

Jensen, Eric. (2003). *Tools for Engagement*. San Diego, CA: The Brain Store.

Jensen, F. E., & Nutt, A. E. (2015). *The teenage brain: A neuroscientist's survival guide to raising adolescents and young adults.* HarperCollins Publishers.

Khalsa, S. B. (2012). *Your brain on yoga*. Cambridge, MA: Harvard University.

Khalsa, S. B., Hickey-Schultz, L., Cohen, D., Steiner, N., & Cope, S. (2012). Evaluation of the mental health benefits of yoga in a secondary school: A preliminary randomized controlled trial. *Journal of Behavioral Health Services & Research,* 39(1), 81–90.

Klein, M., & Guest-Jelley, A. (2014). *Yoga and body image: 25 personal stories about beauty, bravery & loving your body.* Woodbury, MN: Llewellyn Publications.

Kroger, J. (2005). *Identity in Adolescence: The Balance Between Self and Other* (3rd ed.). Psychology Press. Routledge.

Kuehnert, M. (Producer), & Wills, A. (Director). (2012). Partner yoga for teens [DVD]. United States: Shanti Generation.

O'Reilley, M. R. (1998). Radical presence: Teaching as contemplative practice. Portsmouth, NH: Boynton.

Oswalt, Angela. (2015) The development of gender identity. C. E. Zupanick, Psy.D. (Ed.). Retrieved 3/5/15, 9:44 PM from http://www.sevencounties.org/poc/view_doc.php?type=doc&id=41177&cn=1310

Rosenberg, M. (1965). *Society and adolescent self-image*. Princeton, NJ: Princeton University Press.

Siegel, D. (2014). *Brainstorm, the power and purpose of the teenage brain*. New York: Tarcher.

Spear, L. P. (2000). The adolescent brain and age-related behavioral manifestations. *Neuroscience & Biobehavioral Reviews,* 24(4), 417–463.

Spence, J., & Hyde, A. M. (2012). Train-the-trainer: A white paper on the delivery of district-wide yoga education in Pittsburgh, PA. Pittsburgh, PA: Yoga in Schools. Retrieved from http://yogainschools.org/wp-content/uploads/2008/11/yis-white-paper-final-april-2012.pdf

Steinberg, L. (2008). *Adolescence.* New York: McGraw-Hill.

CONCLUSION

This publication is the culmination of over a year of editing material generated and worked on by 23 contributors and 4 reviewers. The yoga instructors, classroom teachers, yoga program leaders, researchers, and school administrators who contributed to this book represent many years of collective experience working with yoga, with children, and with yoga in schools. When we started this work, our goal was to create a useful resource that could inform the many excellent training programs that already exist for school based yoga, support individual instructors throughout their teaching career (and help them choose a training program wisely), and help administrators and classroom teachers make decisions about how to include yoga in their schools most effectively and sustainably. This document is not intended to replace training and certification for yoga instructors, nor is it meant to be used as a training manual.

We worked to bring together individuals with diverse experiences and perspectives to contribute to this book, and this publication would not have been possible without everyone involved. As we complete this particular White Book, we are aware that a gathering of 23 *different* experts might have brought about a different set of best practices that would have been of equal value to the field. For example, if we had had a greater concentration of Physical and Occupational Therapists in our collaboration, more suggestions about particular physical postures might have been present in this book. There is important work to be done to map out exactly this sort of understanding. It is important that we seek greater understanding of the physiological impact of specific yoga practices on children of different developmental stages and abilities. It is our hope that in a few years time, another gathering can re-evaluate this publication, add suggestions that are currently not represented, and revise suggestions based on new experiences and research.

The process of creating this white book itself has been a transformative step for the field of yoga in schools. As we stand at this important crossroads, book in hand, we also wish to share a few observations for those working in the field to consider, especially regarding the need for ongoing collaborative work.

- There are many fields that contextualize our work (e.g., education, neuroscience, developmental psychology, physical and occupational therapy, organizational management, social justice). To be most effective, we need to remain aware of and in relationship with people in these fields. Interdisciplinary research that considers the many factors that might affect outcomes in programming (e.g., school culture, organizational willingness, teacher buy-in, social justice issues) would be helpful.

- Concise definitions for a number of terms are important. We need to stay in communication with each other and work toward agreed-upon (and secular) definitions for words that are commonly used (e.g., yoga, meditation, transformation), and encourage consistency in their use.

- We need each other, as a community, for individual sustainability and greater accountability. This requires us to connect and communicate so we avoid assumptions about the field, the practices, and one another.

- The field would benefit from research that helps us understand what practices are safe and effective for what age groups and at what frequency and duration. For example, is breath retention safe for young children, and if so, how much? What duration of focused attention practice is effective for children in which age groups? What poses may not be safe for children at various developmental stages?

- Although secularism is essential to offering yoga in schools, there is not consensus regarding what this concretely means, either in the yoga in schools field or more broadly. We need to have more conversations about this to find greater clarity and consistency.

- There is much that yoga in schools can learn from the related fields of mindfulness in education and social and emotional learning (SEL). We should support and encourage conversations and relationships between these communities.

Perhaps as important as any of the individual best practices, or the considerations above, is the recognition that teaching yoga in schools, at its best, is never an individual pursuit. It requires, above all, a commitment to cultivating honest and respectful relationships — with children, with teachers and administrators, with other yoga instructors, with parents — and a commitment to seeking ongoing education and support. When we are in a position of power over the bodies, hearts and minds of young people (as all adults working in education are), the standards we set for ourselves must be high and the willingness to keep learning must be strong.

It is our hope that this book is the beginning of something all of us involved in the field can continue to create together: something that ultimately creates more space in our schools for young people to explore practices that support them to balance their emotions, to build confidence, to navigate challenges, and to nurture themselves for a lifetime.

CONTRIBUTOR INFORMATION

Editors and Contributing Editors

Traci Childress, MA, began studying yoga and mindfulness in 1996 and is a founding member of the Yoga Service Council. She is Co-founder of the Children's Community School in West Philadelphia, where mindfulness is a core component of the curriculum (ages 2-6) as well as of her *Teacher Reflection and Mindful Development* program for educators. As founder of the Mindful Reflection Project, she offers workshops, facilitation, curriculum development support, and consulting to educators, schools, nonprofit organizations, and yoga communities.

Jennifer Cohen Harper, MA, E-RCYT, is a leading voice in the children's yoga and mindfulness community, and author of *Little Flower Yoga for Kids: A Yoga and Mindfulness Program to Help Your Child Improve Attention and Emotional Balance*. She is the founder of Little Flower Yoga and The School Yoga Project, the vice president of the Yoga Service Council, and an active member of the International Association of Yoga Therapists. Harper lives in Croton on Hudson NY with her husband and their tiny teacher, Isabelle May.

Adi Flesher, M.Ed., is Director of the Garrison Institute's Contemplative Teaching and Learning Initiative and has more than 20 years of experience in education. He served as assistant director of Camp Tel Yehudah and has developed/run programs to help teens, young adults, and educators understand their own brains and minds. Flesher is currently an adjunct instructor in Counseling, Leadership, Literacy and Special Education at Lehman College, CUNY. He received a M.Ed. in Mind, Brain and Education (Harvard Graduate School of Education) and a dual B.A. in Political Science/Jewish History (Columbia University and the Jewish Theological Seminary).

Argos Gonzalez is an English teacher at a Bronx transfer high school and an adjunct lecturer at Hunter College. He has introduced mindful practices to educators and students and facilitates mindful workshops and meditation classes. Since completing Mindful Schools' yearlong certification and Little Flower Yoga's Level 1 and 2 trainings, he has become interested in the impact of yoga and mindfulness on teachers and students. His dissertation will be on the impact of mindfulness practice on teacher effectiveness.

Andrea Hyde, PhD, is an assistant professor in Educational and Interdisciplinary Studies at Western Illinois University. She teaches courses in the social foundations of education, education policy, and qualitative research; studies school-based yoga curricula and teacher training programs, and has developed mindfulness pedagogy for post-secondary education. A consultant/evaluator for Yoga in Schools (Pittsburgh), Dr. Hyde helps design and deliver a professional development program for using yoga in PE and Health classes. She is also a certified yoga teacher and in Yoga Ed° "Tools for Teachers" workshops.

Wynne Kinder has taught in private and urban public schools for 17 years and, more recently, for nine years in special and alternative education. She specializes in addressing student needs, building relationships, engaging students and teachers, guiding behavior, and teaching attention, social skills and emotional regulation. Kinder has created and taught "Wellness Works in Schools™" for 10 years, is a partner in Kinder Associates LLC and lead instructor (PreK-12), and serves as an educational/mindfulness consultant across the US with Health Teacher (Tennessee).

Contributors

Candy Blaxter is a Certified YogaKids Teacher and Foundations Trainer whose trainings include Radiant Child, Yoga 4 Classrooms, Street Yoga, and Connected Kids. She received her RYT200 in 2010 and is currently enrolled in an RYT500 program. Blaxter has taught yoga and led teacher trainings in Haiti and co-founded the Bridge of Diamonds Haiti Relief Effort in 2010. She also serves on the Board of Go Give Yoga and teaches YogaKids classes in Massachusetts and Maine.

Bethany Butzer, PhD, is a postdoctoral research fellow at Brigham and Women's Hospital, Harvard Medical School in Dr. Sat Bir Khalsa's lab. Butzer directs research on the Kripalu Yoga in the Schools program to evaluate yoga's effect on child and adolescent mental health. An author, speaker and yoga teacher, Butzer's research background spans several areas of Positive Psychology.

Lily Cavanagh is currently a graduate student in Early Childhood Special and General Education at Bank Street College of Education. She is also a 200-hour certified Children's Yoga Teacher through Color Me Yoga® and leads a kids' yoga summer camp in Philadelphia. She has taught yoga in a variety of service settings, including a rehabilitation center and at-risk youth programs.

Cheryl Crawford is the Cat on the Mat. Founder of the Atlanta Yoga Movement, she has spent over a decade fusing Dr. Seuss and other children's books with yoga sutras to help kids find peace, poise and playfulness in everyday life. Crawford worked as an elementary school teacher, reading specialist, and curriculum coordinator in Atlanta for 11 years, and, since giving birth to triplet daughters, has paired her newfound dedication to yoga with her passion for books and teaching.

Anne Desmond is a NYC yoga instructor and co-founder and Executive Director of Bent On Learning, an organization that brings yoga into NYC public schools and integrates health and happiness into education. She organizes and engages board members, volunteers, and donors to further Bent On Learning's mission, and she developed their yoga curriculum for grades 6–12 with Jennifer Ford and Courtney McDowell. She is honored to collaborate with the Yoga Service Council.

Lisa Flynn, E-RYT, RCYT, is the founder of ChildLight Yoga® and Yoga 4 Classrooms®, organizations providing secular, accessible, sustainable yoga and mindfulness-based education in schools, communities, educators, and related professionals. She is a trainer, speaker, and consultant in yoga for children, yoga in schools, and business and personal sustainability. She published *Yoga 4 Classrooms Card Deck* (2011) and *Yoga for Children* (2013).

Lynea Gillen, MS, LPC, RYT200, is the cofounder of Yoga Calm®, a counselor with Portland's The Children's Program, and adjunct faculty at Portland State University. A yoga practitioner since 1973 with over 30 years of experience as a schoolteacher and counselor, she is a licensed professional counselor and coauthor of *Yoga Calm for Children*. She has trained over 1,000 schoolteachers, yoga teachers, parents, and counselors in Yoga Calm, and presented Yoga Calm for Children in several states.

Mayuri Gonzalez is a certified Vinyasa and children's yoga teacher. She began studying yoga, meditation, and mindfulness over 20 years ago and serves as the Director of The School Yoga Project (Little Flower Yoga), bringing staff trainings and yoga and mindfulness classes to the Greater NYC Area. She lives in Westchester County with her husband and two loving little yogis, Naiya and Akin.

Debby Kaminsky is a former advertising executive. A yoga instructor since 2004, she is passionate about helping to manifest positive change. In 2009, she founded the Newark Yoga Movement, which has shared yoga with 15,000+ students, 1,600+ educators, and the Newark community, including nearly 600 firefighters, and inspired the Atlanta Yoga Movement and Indy Yoga Movement. Kaminsky served as Peace Ambassador for the Global Mala NJ and organized all yoga at Newark's 2011 Peace Summit with the Dalai Lama. She has taught yoga in Kenya, Tanzania, and Israel.

Michelle Kelsey Mitchell's ten years of work in public schools in Northern Virginia and Buffalo, NY, have made her aware of the need for early cultivation of self-awareness and that yoga can help children and adults reach their fullest potential. Her yoga training and practice have taught her to appreciate yoga in traditional and modern forms for practitioners of all ages and to fully experience patience, love, and joy. She has a Master's in Counseling & Human Services and an undergraduate degree in Sports Medicine.

Carol Kennedy is a New York City public high school science teacher. She has been teaching environmental education in the South Bronx to at-risk teens for over 20 years. She and her colleagues are developing curricula that use mindful practices in advisory group, science, and English classes.

Sat Bir Singh Khalsa, PhD, is an assistant professor of medicine at Harvard Medical School in the department of sleep medicine at Brigham and Women's Hospital. His projects have focused on the therapeutic applications of yoga in a number of settings, including public schools, and for several conditions, including insomnia, performance anxiety, and PTSD. Dr. Khalsa is one of the most active, skillful, and experienced researchers in the yoga world today.

Dee Marie is the creator and director of CALMING KIDS, a nonprofit offering school yoga programs and teacher trainings since 2004 and winner of the 2013 National Health Awareness Promotions Award from the AMA. Marie has a master's degree in Child and Motor Development from NYU and has worked as a yoga therapist for 28 years, trained by Shri Swami Rama and Mukunda Stiles. Marie is Colorado's SAVE (Stop America's Violence Everywhere) representative.

Allison Morgan, MA, OTR, RYT, is a pediatric occupational therapist and a registered Yoga Alliance teacher. She has been working with children of all abilities for over 25 years in hospital, school and home settings. As the founder of Zensational Kids, LLC, she has developed innovative programs for schools, integrating yoga and mindfulness into curriculums. She consults and conducts workshops and trainings internationally and is a national teacher trainer for the Radiant Child Yoga Program.

Iona M. Smith, MEd, CYT 500, is Program Leader for Kripalu Yoga in the Schools (KYIS) with the Institute for Extraordinary Living. She is co-creator of the KYIS curriculum, co-facilitator of KYIS teacher trainings, and a yoga educator in KYIS research studies. Iona holds a master's degree in education from Harvard University and a 500-hour yoga teacher's certification from the Nosara Yoga Institute in Costa Rica.

Joanne Spence is a social worker, yoga teacher, and international speaker/trainer for health and wellness. She brings 20 years of social work experience to her work in schools and hospitals to empower and motivate teachers through self-care and self-awareness. The Director of Yoga on the Square (Pittsburgh), she is founder and Executive Director of Yoga in Schools and works part-time at Western Psychiatric Institute and Clinic as yoga teacher/staff developer. Joanne is married and is the mother of three lively teenagers.

Vanessa C.L Weiner founded the ResilientKids to offer an integrated, year-round yoga and mindfulness curriculum for students at high-need schools, building emotional intelligence to support academic achievement. She recently completed a chapter for the book *Mindfulness with Youth: From the Clinic to the Classroom* and has presented at conferences on yoga, mindfulness, and stress. She can be found leading workshops for teachers, administrators and students of education, facilitating yoga-art summer camps, and playing with her greatest teachers, her two children.

Reviewers

Carol Horton Ph.D., is the author of *Yoga Ph.D.: Integrating the Life of the Mind and the Wisdom of the Body,* and co-editor of *21st Century Yoga: Culture, Politics, and Practice.* She serves as a Board member with the Yoga Service Council, Advisor to the Yoga and Body Image Coalition, and teacher with Yoga for Recovery. An ex-political science professor, Carol holds a doctorate from the University of Chicago, and is the author of *Race and the Making of American Liberalism.*

Patricia Jennings, M.Ed., Ph.D. is an Associate Professor of Education at the Curry School of Education at the University of Virginia. She is an internationally recognized leader in the fields of social and emotional learning and mindfulness in education. Dr. Jennings is leading the development of the Compassionate Schools Project integrated health curriculum that combines social and emotional learning, mindfulness, nutrition and yoga, which is being evaluated in Louisville, Kentucky. She is the author of Mindfulness for Teachers: Simple Skills for Peace and Productivity in the Classroom.

Sat Bir Singh Khalsa, Ph.D., is an assistant professor of medicine at Harvard Medical School in the department of sleep medicine at Brigham and Women's Hospital. His projects have focused on the therapeutic applications of yoga in a number of settings, including public schools, and for several conditions, including insomnia, performance anxiety, and PTSD. Dr. Khalsa is one of the most active, skillful, and experienced researchers in the yoga world today.

Cynthia Zurchin, Ph.D., is an educator and coach with over 30 years of experience in urban and suburban schools who is not afraid to push in a new direction to achieve success. She has effectively implemented yoga programs in schools reducing student suspensions and increasing student engagement. Cynthia is passionate about improving school culture. She is also the co-author of *The Whale Done School*. Cynthia continues to be a guest lecturer and speaker at seminars and workshops across the United States.

ABOUT OMEGA

Located on more than 200 acres in the beautiful Hudson Valley, Omega Institute for Holistic Studies welcomes more than 23,000 people to its workshops, conferences, and retreats in Rhinebeck, New York, and at other exceptional locations around the world.

Founded in 1977 by Stephan Rechtschaffen, MD, and Elizabeth Lesser, Omega was inspired by scholar and Eastern meditation teacher, Pir Vilayat Inayat Khan. Together, they envisioned a dynamic "university of life" designed to foster an integrated approach to personal growth and social change. The name "Omega" came from the teachings of Pierre Teilhard de Chardin, a renowned 20th-century philosopher, who used the term "Omega Point" to describe the peak of unity and integration toward which all life is evolving.

As a nonprofit organization, Omega has consistently been at the forefront of human development. From nurturing early dialogues on integrating modern medicine and natural healing; to laying the groundwork for new lifestyles and traditions; to designing programs that connect science, spirituality, and creativity; Omega continues to be a place where people from all walks of life come for inspiration, restoration, and new ideas.

Today, our mission guides us to help people find health, happiness, and community while living gently on the Earth.

ABOUT THE YOGA SERVICE COUNCIL

The Yoga Service Council (YSC) was formed in 2009 at the Omega Institute by a group of committed yoga service organizations and their leaders, and has expanded to include 75 global organizations and hundreds of individual members and supporters. In addition, the Council has produced four annual conferences, and published two volumes of the Journal of Yoga Service.

Mission: To maximize the effectiveness, sustainability, and impact of individuals and organizations working to make yoga and mindfulness practices equally accessible to all.

Vision: A world where everyone has equal access to yoga and mindfulness practices that support healing, resilience, self-development, community building and positive social change.

Focus Areas: The Council provides leadership to individuals and organizations working to make yoga and mindfulness practices equally accessible to all. To bring this to life, the YSC serves in five core areas:

1. *Annual Yoga Service Conference at Omega*—Since 2012, experts in the fields of social service, trauma healing, medicine, education, yoga, and mindfulness have gathered to collaborate at Omega and expand knowledge in the field.

2. *Support for City- and College-Based Yoga Service Networks*—The YSC is developing its capacity to serve as the central hub of support and connection for regional- and college-based yoga service networks, as well as fostering the development of new partner organizations both nationally and internationally.

3. *Publication of Best Practice "White Books"*—The YSC publishes an annual series of best practice guides, the first of which is this book, *Best Practices for Yoga in Schools.* The Best Practices for Yoga for Veterans working meeting was held at Omega Institute in October 2015, and the second book in the series is scheduled for publication in the fall of 2016.

4. *Publication of "White Paper" resource guides and issues briefs*—Beginning in 2016 the YSC will launch a new series of "White Papers" to guide reflection, discussion, and learning on critical topics in the field, such as exploring the meaning of "yoga service," working with trauma-informed yoga methods, developing college-based yoga service networks, etc.

5. *Fostering of Collaborative Relationships*—The Council, its Board and members maintain collaborative relationships with universities, national organizations, service providers, and a wide range of professionals in an effort to exchange ideas and support interdisciplinary conversations.

CPSIA information can be obtained
at www.ICGtesting.com
Printed in the USA
LVHW010848270620
659147LV00032B/2097